EYE WITH A VIEW

EYE WITH A VIEW

AMLA MEHTA

This book is not intended as a substitute for the medical advice of physicians. The reader should regularly consult a physician in matters relating to his/her health and particularly with respect to any symptoms that may require diagnosis or medical attention.

The author has tried to recreate events, locales, and conversations from her memories of them. In order to maintain their anonymity, in some instances the author has changed the names of individuals and places, or may have changed some identifying characteristics and details such as physical properties, occupations, and places of residence.

Print ISBN: 978-1-63337-331-0
E-book ISBN: 978-1-63337-332-7
LCCN: 2019914340

Book design and production by
Columbus Publishing Lab
47 N. 4th Street, Suite 204
Zanesville, OH 43701
www.columbuspublishinglab.com

Amla encourages you to contact her.
You can like her Facebook page here: www.facebook.com/Amlainspires
Or email her here: amlalights@gmail.com

Printed in the United States of America

CONTENTS

DEDICATION

I dedicate this book to God. Thank you for giving me great inner-strength and courage to create this inspirational piece of written art and the opportunity to share my heart with the world. And of course, I thank you, God, for this sacred and blessed life.

I dedicate this book to Mom, Dad and Parul. Thank you for allowing me to be open, honest, and write about you. Ha! I love you.

I dedicate this book to Niranjana Mehta, my late *Masi* (aunt) who passed away in 2011.

I dedicate this book to the late S.N. Goenka Ji, my meditation guru and teacher.

I dedicate this book to my dear friend Kalpen Upadhay. You will always be treasured within my heart.

I dedicate this book to ALL the disabled and terminally ill, and to ALL who are in chronic pain and suffering to survive each and every day.

I dedicate this book to all of humanity. We are all connected and united as ONE.

Blessings,
Amla Mehta

INTRODUCTION
Top Ten Perks of Being Legally Blind

10. I won't be obliged to physically see myself getting old with the crinkles and wrinkles.

9. Short lines at airports all over the world.

8. I hear everything. Speak at your own risk around Amla Mehta. Ha!

7. I don't have to see irritated looks on people's faces if I accidentally bump into them in public.

6. I see perfectly inside-out!

5. You don't need vision to sleep at night.

4. I embody a crystal clear and deeper understanding of myself by living with low vision. With that, I am compassionate and I empathize with those who are struggling in the world.

3. Sharp memory skills.

2. Strong intuition.

The number one perk of being legally blind...

By living in the physical dark, I wholeheartedly know that I am the infinite being of Light.

A MESSAGE FROM AMLA MEHTA

From my heart to yours.
If I could help one person like yourself, my true purpose has
been served. Shine Love, Shine Light, Shine You!

Important Disclaimers

1. The exercises that I offer immediately after each story are merely suggestions. Nobody is obligated to do any of these recommended exercises. These particular exercises I offer are what worked for me. Maybe they might help you? Listen to your own intuition and do what feels right for you when testing out these exercises. After all, you are the pilot of your own individual life. Good luck!

2. All stories within *Eye with a View* are true. However, some of the names of people mentioned by Amla Mehta have been changed to protect their own privacy.

Sweet Sixteen, or Was It?

In December of 1989, I had just turned sixteen years old. I was in biology class when the principal's office called my teacher, Mrs. Donnelly, requesting that I head up there after class. Suddenly, my ears felt piping hot, while my nerves electrified my body. This was a usual "Amla response," assuming the worst and thinking I was in deep trouble. Needless to say, I was always the person who worried about being worried.

When the bell rang, I frantically ran up to the principal's office. When I approached the counter, there they lay: sixteen rich, velvety-red, long-stem roses, just for me. I was so pleased, yet perplexed. I thought to myself, *Who gave me these beautiful, breathtaking flowers?*

It was routine for my mom to drive me to and from school. Therefore, when she picked me up, I couldn't resist showing her my pleasant surprise.

I scrammed out the door to the car, carrying these delicate florets of love. It's as if I were holding a precious baby in one arm, while carrying a boulder load of books in my neon-pink backpack over my other shoulder. I approached the car with my mouth hanging wide open, and my big brown eyes must have been the size of quarters; I was so psyched. Mom greeted me with a contagious smile, and just from the look on her face, I instantly knew she was the culprit behind this heartwarming gesture.

Two months later, around Valentine's Day, I had an appointment for an all-day, in-depth eye exam at the Massachusetts Eye and Ear Infirmary in Cambridge, Massachusetts. Apparently, it is the third-highest rated institution of its type in the United States. Nonetheless, I would rather have been learning about the Civil War in history class than go to another meticulous eye appointment. Who the heck wants to spend all day at the doctor's office two hours away from home?

During the drive to the Massachusetts Eye and Ear Infirmary, I had a major flashback to when I visited Dr. Wheeler's office a few months prior to my sixteenth birthday. It was a standard eye checkup with my ophthalmologist, whom I had visited since I was five years old. During this eye exam, he dilated both of my eyes and noticed that my retinas, located deep within the back pocket of the eyes, were abnormal. Yet, Dr. Wheeler couldn't hypothesize an exact reason as to why my eyes were atypical. However, he was certain that my eyes were distinctively distorted and pale in color. Normal retinas are smooth and bright orange/red in color with no scar-like marks.

"I can see there is something quite different with Amla's eyes," he said to my mom and me. "You need to take her to an accredited retina specialist."

Dr. Wheeler directed me to another eye specialist in Hartford, Connecticut, who thoroughly examined my eyes with a series of tests. Unfortunately, this other retina specialist couldn't confirm a definitive diagnosis that explained how and why my eyes were so "different." He then urged us to schedule an appointment with Dr. Berson, a retina specialist in Boston, Massachusetts. A few days later, my mom called Dr. Berson to schedule an appointment.

Which brings me back to February 1990. My parents and I trekked a long, dreadful drive to see Dr. Berson. While my mom drove, I stared out the window, almost in a trance, gazing at the cars as they whipped on by. All I wanted to do was retreat back home, crawl into my cozy ole bed, pull the warm covers over my head, and call it a day.

Prior to my appointment with Dr. Berson, and as part of my diagnostic process, we had been told to set up an appointment with Dr. Shih, a pediatrics genetic nutritionist at the Massachusetts General Hospital. To our pleasant surprise, the office was within walking distance of the Massachusetts Eye and Ear facility.

Our appointment with Dr. Shih was scheduled at 10:00 a.m., giving us ample time to reach our destination, or so we thought. Due to the heavy volume of morning traffic, in addition to Mom having extreme difficulty finding a vacant parking spot when we arrived at the hospital, we were all on edge and in utter distress.

To make matters worse, I was fidgety because Dr. Shih instructed me to fast for twelve hours before having blood drawn, meaning I hadn't eaten anything since the night before. Therefore, I felt faint and famished.

As my parents and I entered the Massachusetts General Hospital, I felt like my shoulders kissed my ears, and I had a gut feeling that this was NOT a normal visit to the eye doctor.

Of course not. *Why was I instructed to see a genetic nutritionist by my ophthalmologist? How does a genetic doctor have any direct connection to my so-called vision issues?*

After waiting for what seemed like an eternity at Dr. Shih's office, the technician finally led me into a room by myself, where she would draw blood. I vividly remember her struggling to catch a "good vein" so she could stick me with that heavy-sized needle. When she finally found a decent vein, the needle slithered its way through my tender blood vessels. What a wonderful reminder of how real, ugly, and horrific this whole process was.

I recall the rush of blood gushing relentlessly into tube after tube like it happened yesterday. I thought to myself, *Gosh darn it, how many tubes of blood do they need from me? Is this ever going to stop?*

Apparently Dr. Shih and her staff were drawing blood to detect if I had a specific genetic condition. Therefore, they were determined to find scientific proof behind any possible physical disorder. I was queasy and nearly ready to pass out considering there was so much blood drawn. I begged for crackers and ginger ale or anything to keep me sane and revitalized.

After I gulped down the entire can of ginger ale, Dr. Shih explained that next she would take a skin biopsy from my lower back for more extensive genetic testing. So, once again, I was pricked with another massive needle in order to numb my entire back and undergo a full biopsy.

As I sat up, Dr. Shih injected the needle. The burning sting penetrated my whole spine. Shortly after, I could feel and hear Dr. Shih make the incision, yet I was pain-free because of the numbing shots. Soon after, they bandaged me up and guided me back into the waiting area.

SWEET SIXTEEN, OR WAS IT?

A few minutes later, Dr. Shih greeted my parents and explained how her team would most likely have the results of the blood work completed by the end of the day. Meanwhile, she instructed my parents and me to move forward and visit Dr. Berson's office.

I glanced at my watch, and sure enough, we were delayed for our appointment with the ophthalmologist. Dr. Shih called Dr. Berson's office immediately and explained the reason behind our tardiness. Despite her call, my parents and I felt flustered as we scurried over to the Massachusetts Eye and Ear Infirmary.

I had a gut feeling this would be a horrendous and strenuous action-packed day of back-to-back eye exams. And being there point-blank sucked.

The technicians seemed cordial enough and aided me from one room to the other; I took a regular eye chart test, color tests, dark adaptation test, and electroretinography test (known as an ERG). To top it all off, the team of technicians took photographs of my retina, which would help confirm the physical condition of my eyes.

One of the most crucial examinations I experienced was the peripheral vision test. For this procedure, the technician placed a patch over one eye. Next, I was guided to move my head forward into this circular white dome where my lower jaw stood still and aligned on a chin rest. The technician then instructed me to gaze toward the pinpoint hole located within the center of the dome. Then, he displayed a light for me to detect from the outer edges of the dome, gradually moving inward toward the center pinpoint hole.

As soon as I saw the light from the corner of my eye, I was required to press a button using a joint stick so the technician could record accurate data.

Each eye took approximately thirty to forty minutes to examine, which consisted of sifting through at least three different types of light. These ranged from the size of a penny to the size of a pencil eraser, down to the size of a pinhole light. The latter danced around the dome for me to find like the "Where's Waldo" puzzle. This was only my first test, and I was wiped out already.

After the peripheral vision test, I then took a dark adaptation test. This test surveys the eye functionality within pitch-black darkness. First, the technician dilated my eyes by drizzling three drops within each eye. This step alone was agonizing. Almost immediately my eyes burned in intense pain. Nevertheless, I teared up partially because of the drops, but primarily because of my wavering emotions washing over my core being.

Why am I here? Why is all of this testing causing me so much physical and emotional pain and suffering?

I fought the tears rolling down my face because I was brave and strong. And in my mind, the strong don't cave in and weep like a baby. I was a warrior woman on the battlefield, despite these transformational circumstances. Therefore, I courageously followed the procedures set forth by the technicians and doctors at the facility.

The most exasperating part of the entire day was when the doctors dilated my eyes prior to examining my retina. Essentially, I felt like I was looking through waves of water to identify something at the bottom of a swimming pool; everything was unidentifiable and blurry beyond recognition. Unfortunately, these series of tests at Dr. Berson's office were far from over.

After dilating both eyes, the technician placed bandages over each eye in order for me to be fully engulfed in darkness. The main purpose for this test was to evaluate how my retinas functioned in the dark.

The wait time of being in the dark, with my parents directly beside me, was at least thirty minutes. This particular test takes approximately an hour to test both eyes, depending on each patient.

As a metaphor, the retina represents the film of a 1960s camera. If there is no film in the camera, there is no picture. Hence, without a healthy retina, there is no sensory projection of stimuli for the eye to scan and detect light floating in or floating out (basically no external "picture"). This was fresh and new in my mind because ironically enough, I was learning about the parts of the eye in Mrs. Donnelly's biology class.

After being at the facility for a good chunk of the day, there was nothing else to do but contemplate the anticipated results and the status of my eyes. I'd never had such in-depth eye tests in my entire life, and this was way too blistering for my sixteen-year-old self.

Furthermore, the gauntlet of eye tests forced me to assume that my chances of having a positive outcome were slim. As a result, my heart felt heavy, and I felt my stomach churn and emit loud gurgling noises.

As soon as my dark adaptation test was over, the technician ripped off those bandages from my eyes. We both then headed back to the waiting room where I sat with my parents again. Soon after, I took extensive color tests, scanning an array of hues from pale in color to dark in color. I also took an ERG test, which objectively tested the functionality of my eyes 24 hours a day. Lastly, I underwent a series of photographs of my eyes. No fail, this process alone was the most brutal segment of the whole day. That is, my eyes were already excessively dilated; I was experiencing severe glare issues and astigmatism. As a result, not only was I physically fatigued, but the beaming flash from the camera made me feel blinded by the lights.

Shortly after taking those eye photographs, once again I was directed to return to the waiting area.

While growing up, it was "normal" for my parents to be protective of my sister and me. However, as we waited for the doctor to announce my name, I noticed my parents acting even more guarded than usual. It was like they didn't want me engaging with any of the other patients. I assumed it was because the others might reveal something I wasn't ready to hear, sitting in that tiny closet space of a waiting area. However, I swallowed my nagging thoughts and continued to bore myself by staring at the ground.

In hindsight, I instinctively knew my parents were wearily concerned for my overall well-being. They, too, were petrified of the real-life nightmare that might be in store for their sixteen-year-old daughter.

I am not a parent. That being said, I can only imagine witnessing my own child going through eye doctors like tissue paper, year after year, ever since he or she was five years old.

Dr. Berson then flagged my parents into his office. As I waited, ten minutes slid into fifteen minutes, which slammed into thirty minutes. I thought to myself: *Why is this consultation taking so long?*

It was approximately 4:00 p.m., and at this time there was a high possibility of a lengthy ride home because of the evening rush-hour traffic. I yearned to hit the road. Heck, I had just turned sixteen and was super excited to earn my driver's license.

If I only had my driver's license that particular day, I

would've been so tempted to ditch those doctors and drive home independently.

Mom and Dad finally exited Dr. Berson's office. Seeing their blank stares, I was confused and couldn't suspect what the ophthalmologist had revealed. The doctor then asked all three of us to join him in his office.

It was somewhat dark when we all entered the room. My parents sat in two chairs next to the door, facing me as I adjusted myself into the eye exam chair. I was literally sitting on the edge of my seat.

Everything that happened next was a big blur for me. I remember talking to Dr. Berson about the results of each eye exam. However, oddly enough, he didn't mention any details on the possible prognosis and status of my eyes. I thought that was strange, since Dr. Berson had consulted with my parents for such an extended amount of time. However, I was bushed, and I so badly wanted to flee and journey back home. Minutes later, we officially wrapped up the vision consultation and exchanged our goodbyes.

At the last minute, the technician gave me complimentary plastic sunglasses to protect my eyes from the glare outside, especially from the headlights of oncoming traffic on the opposite side of the highway. Just to reiterate, my eyes were highly sensitive to bright and shiny lights due to the daunting, prolonged day of eye tests.

"Yippee!" I said sarcastically to the technician when she handed me the glasses. However, I appreciated them ever-so-dearly when I found myself struggling to navigate my way out to the parking lot and into our car.

Attempting to drive home was a complete nightmare. These were the days prior to the birth of the internet and mobile devices.

Therefore, in order to make our way back home, my parents were limited to using road maps or asking for help locally. After all of us settled into our car, within seconds my parents' voices had risen fast into a high-pitch volume as they irritated each other, squabbling over directions.

"Anil, you have to make yourself available and help me find Storrow Drive, and then we'll worry about finding the Massachusetts Turnpike," my mom exclaimed.

Unfortunately, the signs to get back on the highway were crooked and hidden behind bushy landscaping and trees. Therefore, by the time my mom saw the sign to Storrow Drive, the branch highway leading to the Massachusetts Turnpike, we had missed the major turn altogether.

I would've been happy to help my mom if I'd had sharper vision. However, it was winter and dark by 5:00 p.m., so I found it quite burdensome to see or identify anything at all on our way home due to my night blindness.

"Are we ever going to get back home safely?" I whispered quietly to myself as my parents drove around in circles multiple times. To add more fuel to the fire, it was approaching 5:30 p.m., and the steady traffic looked more like a parking lot on the packed highway with several detours due to road construction. And of course, due to the mind-blowing and chaotic traffic, my parents continued ranting and raving while I sat trapped in the backseat with nowhere to escape.

After driving around numerous rotaries, we finally found a well-lit gas station where my mom felt safe enough to exit our automobile and ask for directions. One would assume my father, being the man of the house, would have adamantly urged my mom to stay inside the vehicle, yet he remained quiet and reserved

Growing up, my dad had always been discombobulated when attempting to follow instructions, especially when asking for directions. The words spewing out of anybody trying to help my dad navigate were completely useless, especially if we were lost. Essentially, my dad rarely, or never, absorbed any new information unless it was repeated at least five times. My dad hears people, but he rarely listens to them. As the saying goes, words go in one ear and out the other. Hands down, a non-verbal response is somewhat typical of my father.

Nevertheless, my mom walked over to the gas station attendant and politely asked for directions. And even though we all felt stuck in the spin cycle of confusion, I heard my mom bursting out with laughter as she talked to the gas attendant. My mother was a gentle soul, yet when hardships occurred, she was a lioness-hearted soul. With a soft smile, she calmly returned to the vehicle, and at last we were on our merry way home to western Connecticut.

During the remainder of the drive home, my parents were pin-drop silent, which was unusual. I didn't utter a word. In the Mehta family there was never a dull moment. However, I had no energy to spare by babbling away like I normally did with them. All I wanted was to eradicate that unbearable day and pretend like it never happened.

By the time we reached home, I was burned out. My parents were too, considering they drove for at least five to six hours to and from Boston, in addition to waiting in limbo-land all day long at Dr. Berson's office. I fell asleep in seconds that night, snuggling into my sanctuary bed.

Friday morning, I felt like someone had knocked me out in my own boxing ring. I was clearly not ready to get up for school. Within minutes, I was experiencing double vision and had more glare issues because of the aftermath of those potent eye drops and dilation of the eyes. *Enough of those freaking eye tests*, I consoled myself.

I reluctantly dragged myself out of bed and physically got ready for school but was nowhere near mentally prepared. Furthermore, I was troubled that I would not be able to function normally during class because of the heavy-duty throbbing feeling behind my eyes, along with the added feature of my saucer-sized pupils overpowering my face.

As my mom dropped me off at school, I was that moody teenager, displacing all of my frustrations upon her for no good reason. She gave me a sharp look. "Amla, you're not the only one who feels cranky this morning. Do you know how exhausted your father and I are? We didn't sleep, tossing and turning all night long."

I thought to myself, *Why did they have trouble falling asleep? Weren't they too tired to be restless last night?*

However, I didn't allow this scenario to consume me because I was already running behind by not getting any homework done.

For the next couple of months, everything seemed somewhat normal within our family. However, I sensed something was off with my mom and dad. Especially my dad. He coddled me and acted overly concerned. I found that puzzling because he had never asked about my well-being as often as after that wretched visit to Dr. Berson's office.

Mom was mom. She was the true glue of the family. She lovingly made me feel better, no matter how crabby I acted as a teenager.

In the spring of 1990, I experienced a life-altering change. I vividly remember that it was a mucky and cloudy Sunday afternoon.

SWEET SIXTEEN, OR WAS IT?

My sister, Parul, was home, which was unusual since she was a social butterfly, gallivanting with her friends from college. She was a sophomore and commuted back and forth from home to school. Parul and I were, and still are, polar opposites. She was that cute, petite Indian gal with a ton of friends. And to top it off, young guys were quite fond of her, which made me feel downright jealous.

I was a loner, a quirky sixteen-year-old girl with the red candy-apple "Sally Jessy Raphael" glasses that consumed most of my face. I must admit, I was more like the character Ally Sheedy played in the movie *The Breakfast Club*: awkward, with no social skills, just a girl trying to get by. I enjoyed hanging out by myself, because that was my only way of me being me.

I recall lounging around in my worn-out blue jeans and a faded purple T-shirt on the couch. I don't remember who instigated the argument, but because Parul and I were so freakishly different; we started bickering, which escalated into a reckless shouting match.

I snapped at her. "You're always socializing with your friends, going out to parties and hanging out with the guys. I despise the fact that you're never home, and I am stuck here with Mom and Dad."

She rolled her eyes. "Amla, it's not like I was 'miss life of the party' when I was sixteen. I never went out in high school. I only started being more social in college."

"You always have everybody's attention, young and old. I'm always invisible standing next to you," I exclaimed.

In a New York minute, Parul was triggered, and I suppressed anything she said afterwards. However, I do recall those heart-wrenching words that were jabbered out of her mouth: "Well Amla, it's not my fault you're going blind," she screamed.

I grabbed the aquamarine blanket nearby and pulled it over my head attempting to hide my physical reaction. "Whaaat?" I cried.

My parents, who'd been in the kitchen, ran into the living room and gawked at my sister in sheer astonishment. Parul gasped, placed her hand over her mouth, and stared back at all of us with guilt written all over her face. She then added: "I'm kidding, Amla!"

I wasn't going to allow her to backpedal and erase her words. "No, you're not! I can hear the raw truth in your voice. You are not joking," I exclaimed.

I couldn't believe my ears. I was going blind. Just those words alone haunt me. "Oh my God! My eyes are dying and I won't be able to see at all!" I screeched at the top of my lungs.

I sunk down into the sofa while burying my head even deeper into my blanket. It was only then that I felt secure enough to weep the tears away, and while gasping for air I cried. *Why? Why is this happening to me? I am innocent; I didn't do anything to inflict this upon myself. Why?*

When I peeked out of my "fort blanket," I noticed my parents were rooted to the ground. They, too, were bawling their eyes out as Parul stood there in panic mode. The candid look on her face explained it all: *What have I done? Why did I blurt out those words? I didn't mean any harm.*

But, of course, it was a little too late. She had exposed the pink elephant in the room. The truth was out there for all eyes to see.

My parents' faces were both white as a ghost. What on earth was going through their minds? They knew it was their responsibility to directly explain that their daughter was going blind, yet had not done so.

In hindsight, all the dots figuratively connected as to why my parents were so hyperactive and frazzled during the ride home from the Massachusetts Eye and Ear Infirmary, why my mom experienced serious insomnia, and why my dad deliberately gave me "unnecessary" extra attention. Of course, my parents didn't know how to tell me because they couldn't cope with and comprehend the groundbreaking news for themselves, never mind directly telling their daughter that she's going blind.

And despite my family's distress and discomfort, I felt relieved that Parul had accidentally spilled the beans about my blindness issue. At least the truth had been unleashed. And we, as a united family, had no choice but to move forward together.

In order to help me understand my particular eye disease, my parents eventually handed me some pamphlets that Dr. Berson had given them. Of course, my parents weren't able to explain the exact details of my eye condition as accurately as the information within the pamphlets. However, they tried their very best because they loved me so much and cared for my physical well-being.

I didn't dare to glance at those pamphlets until I was ready and willing to discover that paramount information about my eye disease. So, I scampered off into my pink cotton-candy colored room, my private safe haven, and spread out all the pamphlets along with the eye-test results on my twin-size bed.

I learned that I have an eye disease called Gyrate Atrophy, a genetic disorder in which my peripheral vision gradually fades into tunnel vision over time. The prognosis of blindness occurs between the ages of forty-five and sixty, at which time the majority of my vision would fizzle and corrode away. Only 200 people have been officially diagnosed with Gyrate Atrophy in the world.

When I read this, I thought to myself, *Great, a whole 199 other people are suffering from this monstrous eye disease.*

I also read how Gyrate Atrophy originated in Finland. *Hello? I am 100 percent Indian and an exquisite shade of brown, unlike those northern European people. How did I get this eye condition?*

I was baffled beyond belief.

At sixteen, I wondered if I would ever attend college and read textbooks just like any other student. Would I find a high-quality job and instantly get hired? I was already the weird one; who the heck would want to fall in love or marry a blind lady? These were scary, yet real-life potential hurdles, foreshadowed by what I was reading about my eye condition.

Over the next month or so, because Gyrate Atrophy is a genetic disorder, my sister was also tested through blood work. Fortunately, she does not have the eye condition.

What were my chances of receiving this eye disease? Due to genetics, my parents are both carriers of Gyrate Atrophy but do not suffer from the disease. Genetics 101: because both of my parents are carriers, as their offspring, I had a 25 percent chance of developing Gyrate Atrophy. Despite such low odds, I inherited this rare disorder. And because Gyrate Atrophy is a genetic eye disorder, we still don't know anybody within our extended family who has contracted this particular eye condition. (On a side note, currently, as of 2019, scientists have not developed a test that can predict if parents are carriers of Gyrate Atrophy or not.)

During the next couple of years, Gyrate Atrophy was a constant buzz in my ear. However, vision or no vision, I was still alive and had an abundant life ahead of me. I received my driver's license in 1991, graduated from high school in June of 1992, and the following fall I was admitted and attended the University of Connecticut. Physically, I had no problem reading textbooks throughout my college years. However, going to social gatherings at night was quite challenging to say the least, because I was blind as a bat after nightfall.

In January 1996, my senior year of college, after one of my routine eye checkups, Dr. Wheeler requested that I surrender my driver's license due to the fact that my peripheral vision had been critically compromised.

On that immobilizing day of losing my license, I approached the DMV worker behind the counter and informed her that I was declared legally blind and was no longer permitted to drive. She then demanded I hand over my license immediately.

Within heart thrusting moments, I realized that although I was forced to give up driving, I had zero motivation to manually surrender my physical license to the clerk. This act symbolized key facets of my freedom being downsized forever.

"You don't know how much this license means to me. Can't I keep my physical license as a souvenir?" I cried. "I won't use it to drive; that's illegal anyway."

She looked at me and bluntly said, "No, you must give it up. It's the law."

When I handed over my driver's license, various thoughts flooded through my mind:

I will never, ever be able to drive for the rest of my life.

I can't believe this is unraveling right before me.

Not only am I physically losing my vision, I am forced to lose another precious part of my life, the sweet privilege to drive.

Back when I was able to drive, I felt so liberated and independent. Merely doing errands around town for my mom was an honor. However, from that moment on, I would feel like a little kid, asking for rides to and from places. This would not be smooth sailing either, considering the state of Connecticut had limited options for public transportation.

Despite this jagged disruption, I wholeheartedly believed that being a non-driver would not hinder my personal or professional lifestyle.

After graduating from college in 1996 with a BA in Sociology, a few months later I traveled back to India, solely as a graduation present to myself. My main purpose was to visit extended family and to experience the vast colors, tastes, sounds, and smells of my Indian heritage, authentically, for three months. And being 10,000 miles away from home allowed me to sift through and savor my heart's desires for my next chapter in life. I arrived back to the United States in December of 1996.

In January 1997, my parents nudged me to see another eye specialist since I refused to visit Dr. Berson's office. They too planned a trip to India to visit my grandmother who had failing health. My parents were concerned that I would forgo any eye appointment in their absence. "Amla, you haven't been to Dr. Berson's office since you graduated from high school," my mom said. "You need to get your eyes checked."

Behind closed doors, I hissed at her desperate plea. However, in my heart I knew my mom was right. I hesitated for a few days but then finally set a tentative appointment with good old Dr. Wheeler. Yes, once again I felt flabbergasted—no good news ever resulted after any visit with an eye doctor.

SWEET SIXTEEN, OR WAS IT?

The day of the appointment I scuffed my feet out the door into my parents' hunter-green Honda Civic. After starting the car, feeling all empowered for a whole two seconds, I scooched over to the front passenger seat. As I waited for my mom to get moving, I thought to myself, *Partaking in rides to and from Dr. Wheeler's office is a symbol of my complete dependence on others for the rest of my life.*

Gyrate Atrophy was not only stealing my physical eyes, it was also testing my willpower to soak up my genuine feelings. On the one hand, I somewhat accepted not driving, but on the other, I was battling a war within my inner-self and sustained deep emotional scars.

When we arrived at the doctor's office, I told my mom, "Go do your thing after dropping me off." I was twenty-three, independent, and needed my own space to focus on the next few calculated steps to take pertaining to my eye condition.

Once I entered the examination room, Dr. Wheeler asked if I had been receiving proper care and extensive treatment regarding Gyrate Atrophy.

"What do you mean by that?" I asked.

"Are you routinely going to a qualified eye specialist who treats Gyrate Atrophy patients?" Dr. Wheeler asked.

I felt like he'd opened another skeleton in my closet. *Sure, let's talk about my eyes all day long.* I gritted my teeth and said, "No."

He didn't have a clue as to how I was coping and plowed straight ahead. "Let me put it to you this way. If you were my daughter, I would encourage you to seek treatment in Washington, DC, at the National Institutes of Health," he said. When I didn't respond, he added, "They conduct studies specifically on Gyrate Atrophy patients like yourself, and it's one of the best research institutions in the world."

This was a boatload of information for me to imbibe, as if Dr. Wheeler were taking Gyrate Atrophy to another unpredictable and complex level. I wanted to magically disappear out of my chair. This was a life-changing decision, and I needed to be extremely cautious in order to evaluate the pros and cons of being a participant at this worldwide accredited research institution.

Dr. Wheeler then stalled, implying that I should give him a definitive response to his suggestion. However, I just glared at him until he moved uncomfortably. I finally expressed that I would *think* about being a participant.

With that, we carried forward with the standard eye exam, and an hour later he waved at me out the door and I was off.

On the car ride home, my mom asked me about my appointment with Dr. Wheeler, and I deflected by cranking up the music on the radio.

I wrestled with the idea of being a participant at the NIH for several weeks. And because my parents were out of the country, this was my perfect opportunity to make a rational decision based on my own needs. As a result, I felt compelled to head down to the NIH because Dr. Wheeler's words of wisdom echoed in my mind, "If you were my daughter..."

Several weeks later, I contacted the chief ophthalmologist at the NIH, Dr. Muriel Kaiser. Soon after, I was accepted into the program. The NIH is an internationally acclaimed institution and continues to seek patients like me, since Gyrate Atrophy is such a rare form of an eye disease. Symbolically, I knew I represented their Guinea pig in a lab with the "appropriate eye testing disease" to examine all intricate levels.

On one hand, I felt optimistic for the opportunity to get my eyes thoroughly examined from A to Z. I had hoped that these particular doctors would encourage me to adapt and cope with Gyrate Atrophy on a practical level, since they portrayed themselves as a team of experts. In addition, I had faith and felt blessed to be relatively near the facility, considering people from all over the world visit and become a participant at the NIH.

Unexpectedly, on my flight down to DC in the spring of 1997 with my mom (who was back from India), I felt my optimism disintegrate. Sitting on the airplane and speculating about my upcoming appointment made me feel like I was three years old all over again. Meaning, not being able to gauge when my stomach was full and feeling like vomiting all over myself.

My gut told me that being a patient at the National Institutes of Health would be another gripping experience. And once again, I had those broken-record questions swirling through my mind: *How will I eventually cope without vision? How will I live a decent life being physically disabled? Why me?*

Ever since I was a little girl, I had a strong sense of hope and optimism. And even though I was riled up about having to endure these non-stop, meticulous eye exams, I was confident enough to believe that these doctors were highly qualified to make my five-day stay more at ease. Therefore, I spent the rest of my flight trying to focus on the positive.

Dr. Kaiser's staff hired a driver named Thomas to take Mom and me to and from the airport. When Mom and I exited the baggage claim area, he greeted us with a welcoming smile, and we were off to Bethesda, Maryland, to the NIH. The front desk staff checked us in and assigned Mom and me a room to share. I barely slept, and I was repulsed by the cold, stiff, and uncomfortable hospital bed. I anxiously wondered what these doctors would subject me to in the upcoming days of eye treatment.

The moment I finally fell sound asleep, bam! I was abruptly woken at 6:00 a.m. by the nurse to draw blood. I barely opened my eyes due to being so darn tired.

I clearly recall feeling like a prisoner, and my room represented my jail cell. Because protocol dictated I had a 10 p.m. curfew, there were confining limitations as to when and how long I was allowed to explore Washington, DC. I found these rules and regulations ridiculous.

Who are these people to command any curfew? What are the consequences if I choose to disregard their authority over me? Will they call the police and arrest me?

I was over eighteen and an adult. It was my prerogative when I chose to return to the hospital if I had the desire to go out sightseeing.

All of these ludicrous rules restricted me from being my pure Amla self. And due to my brief internal temper tantrum, I needed to decompress away from my mom to prepare myself mentally and physically for those tedious eye tests. Therefore, I asked my mom to sit back and relax in the hospital room while I moved through each eye test independently.

As you might have guessed already, for the next five days, eight hours a day, it was a continuous heavy-loaded process of prodding and probing by technicians who used ice-cold steel instruments. And when the doctors weren't shining bright lights in my eyes, my vision was considerably obscured since they artificially dilated my pupils almost the entire day for all five days.

During the bulk of the tests, I felt like the walking dead, mindlessly moving from one test room to another. And yes, I went through an extensive and extremely familiar series of eye examinations including: color tests, dark adaptation tests, peripheral vision tests, taking countless photographs of my retina, and lastly, another ERG test, which measured and monitored the functionality of my retina objectively, similarly to how an EKG test monitors the heart.

However, these particular tests were much more advanced and time consuming compared to the tests at Dr. Berson's office. No fail, being a participant at the NIH was much more abrasive than the entire experience at the Massachusetts Eye and Ear Infirmary. Dr. Berson was a sweet peach compared to these indifferent and authoritative doctors and technicians.

I wondered, *Do they really think they're doing me a huge favor having me undergo all of these eye tests? Should I forever be grateful to them?*

One of the most disturbing feelings I endured at the NIH, was that the eye tests magnified the ugly truth of coping with Gyrate Atrophy. Needless to say, by the third night I was a nervous wreck. I remember pulling the blanket around me so tightly as I pleaded with myself: *Haven't I been through enough already?*

And if this wasn't enough, the NIH visit brought back dreadful memories of being forced to surrender my driver's license back in 1996. I felt like an avid runner on a track, jumping over one hurdle after the other, going around in circles with no final destination. I had encountered one too many obstacles. To add more salt to the wound, I wasn't making any significant progress while I chased substantial answers in the ongoing saga of vision loss. As a result, I felt bleak, run-down, and out of my element.

That being said, the majority of my time at the NIH I was dazed and confused because my eyes were so strained and weakened due to lack of sleep, no appetite, and experiencing starbursts of light streaming into my dilated pupils on a daily basis.

Despite my nurturing and loving mother, I still felt isolated, and my emotions were pushing me back and forth like ocean waves crashing against the rocks.

At about 10:00 a.m. on my third day at the NIH, there were at least three or four doctors in what felt like an interrogation room, frequently waving their sophisticated instruments at me. I asked if I could use the bathroom and excused myself. But in all honesty, I needed to escape from being caged at the NIH altogether. I hustled back to my hospital room as my heart pounded out of my chest.

When I entered the room, I must have had a look of sheer desperation. I even startled my mom, who had been watching television. "What happened, Amla?" she asked with concern.

I lost it and burst into tears.

After I calmed down, I explained to my mom what had transpired. She was furious and passionately insisted that she give those doctors a piece of her mind and be that protective mama bear fighting for her baby. However, I was an adult, and this was my personal battle to overcome. After ten or fifteen minutes I composed myself, strutted right back into the room, sat in the chair, and exclaimed, "I need to see a social worker!"

All the doctors glanced at each other and looked at me like I had three heads. "Why do you need a social worker?" asked one.

It took all of my Amla-energy not to pounce at that egotistical technician like a lion salivating at a piece of meat. Frankly, it was none of their business; it was my right as a patient.

And because of my assertiveness, Dr. Kaiser finally agreed and granted me permission to speak with a social worker on the fourth day.

This was my blessed chance to be real and freely let go of my wavering emotions without any resistance. And an added bonus was hopefully connecting with a genuine advocate like a social worker.

Due to the accumulative and disheartening experiences at the NIH, figuratively speaking I felt like I was on house arrest. The doctors were standing on guard like the police patrol car adjacent to a suspect's home. I was even being watched while eating my lunch. Needless to say, my emotions suffocated my human beingness, and I was dying to exhale and release the tension that had amplified throughout my entire stay at the NIH.

When the social worker initially walked into the room, my heart rate slowed down almost immediately. She was there to fully support my emotional and psychological needs. Her wavy salt-and-pepper hair was pulled back in a bun, and her jet-black eyeglasses sat perched on top of her head. She graciously smiled at me, the first person who'd genuinely done so since I had arrived at the NIH. Her appearance itself illustrated that she was ready to dive into our time together.

During our session, I casually said, "It's not like I have cancer or I'm dying. I'm lucky it's only my vision that's the so-called problem."

"No, you're not dying Amla, but you are facing an extreme form of loss," she said.

Those words sliced right through me. I broke down in despair, and tears quickly turned from streams into rivers, relentlessly flowing down my cheeks.

I was facing loss, and I needed to hear the pure truth from somebody who knew the psychological effects of physical and emotional trauma. She inferred that most people at twenty-three wade into life like they would in a swimming pool, taking their time getting adjusted to the water temperature.

"You, Amla, are being forced to dive into the deep end, without having the luxury to adapt to the water temperature or how deep the pool may be. You have no choice but to confront and grieve through gradual vision loss," she said.

"It's not fair!" I cried.

She paused and intentionally waited until I was ready to speak again. We continued our session for the remainder of the hour, until I felt calm and even-tempered. We then exchanged our goodbyes, and she gave me her contact information, telling me to feel free and contact her at any time.

At last I felt heard, empowered, and healed with a counselor who showed me that she sincerely cared. And finally I felt like I was the director and conductor of my life for once, since I have no control over Gyrate Atrophy. More importantly, for the first time in a long time, I felt understood.

On my last day at the NIH, I felt so relieved that my time spent had expired. And because of my distasteful experience, I felt like I was just another number according to Dr. Kaiser and her team of technicians. In my perspective, they were the blind ones, refusing to see the patient's needs of support, care, and compassion.

Frankly speaking, it's paralyzing fearing the unknown outcome of Gyrate Atrophy. However, that reflective conversation with my social worker was one of the most pivotal moments of my life. I needed to hear the underlying truth—the reality of the loss—before I could accept Gyrate Atrophy in totality. Since then, I've realized that it takes time to accept this colossal notion of blindness.

Nonetheless, after returning home from this challenging experience at the NIH, I was motivated to emotionally and mentally work through the inevitable ripple effects of Gyrate Atrophy. However, the Universe wasn't finished throwing some life-sized curveballs in my direction.

Three weeks after my visit to the NIH, my grandmother died in India. And although my mom was heartbroken, she was at peace because she had her final chance to preserve those precious moments with my grandmother in person. Grandma was eighty-six years old and endured multiple complications from pneumonia.

My grandmother's death hit me like a ton of bricks. That being said, I felt like everything around me was dying. In rapid succession, I began to lose adequate parts of my Amla-being: my physical vision, my freedom, my loved ones, and my natural sense of optimism.

Since being diagnosed with Gyrate Atrophy back in 1990, I have collected several gifts of insight along the path of losing my vision. One is: no one is immune from loss. We all move closer to death every second of our lives. However, do we intentionally think about that? Of course not. Although death is a natural part of life, we grow and evolve by setting reasonable goals and aspirations to live a prosperous and meaningful life.

My biggest pet peeve is when people try to make me feel better and say, "Oh, Amla, there are so many people who are legally blind. You are not the only one losing vision."

Of course, I'm not the only blind lady on this planet. Yet, if somebody just lost all of their possessions in a four-alarm fire, how would they feel if I said, "So many people have lost their homes; you're not the only one."

Ultimately, until personal loss impacts your individual life, you genuinely don't understand the full extent of challenges a person faces in such dire situations.

Loss takes many forms. Loss can mean losing your keys, losing your phone, losing your job, losing a loved one. Whether loss is replaceable or not, it still affects your life.

Instead of offering simplistic platitudes, be mindful and compassionate with others who are experiencing any form of loss. After all, nothing is set in stone, and you might find yourself conquering an extreme form of loss yourself, needing some kind of assistance.

Another key element when experiencing loss is the attachment factor—material things tethered to what someone has lost. Large or small, it's tough facing loss when you are physically attached to a prior state of "normalcy."

In my particular case, going from being a driver to losing my driver's license within four years was obviously a drastic form of loss. Being so young, it was a heartbreaking stage of my life, but I overcame and accepted this hardship only through time and maturation. In no way, shape, or form was it easy, however, I survived.

Truth be told, loss never fully subsides. However, eventually the weighted down emotions tapers off if you choose to march on and heal, regardless of the consequences.

In simple terms, the more you become friends with loss, the more you can factor in and assess your attachment level to your particular situation. If you are overly emotional, it might be a true sign that you are excessively attached, and this may deter you away from making mindful decisions.

Please take note, it's okay to feel and experience your emotions. However, once you feel them authentically, whether it be through crying, venting, or exercise, then what? Learn to observe your emotions from a distance by taking a step back and consciously soaking in the experience from an eagle-eye point of view.

Doing this enables you to detach from your loss and be in the present—NOW. Once you are fully present, it's easier to accept what is occurring objectively and with less judgment because all that's guaranteed is here and now. And remember, being present requires great will and practice to absorb each moment for what it is, objectively not subjectively.

Facing loss is a part of the game of life. And participating in the game involves risk. Therefore, sometimes you get hit and fall down, and sometimes you come out strong and on top. Such is life: sometimes you win, sometimes you lose. Regardless, whether you win or lose, there is always something to learn.

Of course, your loss may not be as extreme as mine. Yes, I felt very attached to living a more liberated life when I had full-scale vision. However, any form of loss may still linger on and might negatively impact your true essence if you haven't embraced the loss or challenge itself. Thus, as the saying goes: what you resist, persists.

Losing my vision—which is irreplaceable—forced me to reevaluate, renew and revamp myself as a brand new and improved Amla.

It took me at least a decade to admit to and accept myself as being legally blind. More importantly, as my attitude changed, my whole perspective on facing loss changed for the better. This came into fruition only because I chose to stand up time and time again after every setback and loss.

One of these days I most likely will lose most of my sight. And as a result, I simply won't be able to read, watch TV, or even make a cup of coffee as easily as I do today. However, while being visually impaired might shift and alter my daily routine life, the unconditional love for myself is everlasting.

We will all grow old someday and may be challenged on all levels since the body naturally slows down as we age. That being said, you might reminisce over those simple tasks you once were capable of and now cannot achieve without asking for assistance. Regardless of failing health, aging, or the breakdown of the immune system, it's your own attitude and perspective that paves the way to living a full and fat life.

Loss is loss, and there is nothing I can do to prevent it, especially when suffering from Gyrate Atrophy. However, I can change my attitude and transform it into gratitude. With that, it takes great tenacity to be in complete gratitude for the insurmountable qualities and strengths I embody as a legally blind lady versus the qualities I do not have, like 20/20 vision.

Being legally blind impacts my everyday life, whether I like it or not. However, I believe that everything is not only connected but intertwined. It's like the threads running through a tapestry. I might not have my own choice in the thread's color. However, I have the choice to create my own design with the threads given to me by the universe.

That being said, I could sit around and mope about why I only have this one color of thread to work with, but I don't. My heightened intuition focuses on the intangible qualities I exude, such as hope and faith, unconditional love for myself, self-worth, and insight.

I also have realized the true purpose of my vision loss was for my highest good, even though Gyrate Atrophy is debilitating and a chronic form of pain and suffering.

Yes, I am both flawed and blessed. And if I can accept my loss, more or less, so can you. You just have to be honest with yourself and own it. Be happy with the person you see reflected within a mirror. Because in the end, if you don't like and love yourself, who will?

The exact time frame of when I changed my attitude for the better towards Gyrate Atrophy is tough to pin down, because of the camouflage effects of gradual vision loss. The key exercise that helped me get through each challenge is the Serenity Prayer.

God grant me the Serenity to accept the things I cannot change, the Courage to change the things that I can, and the Wisdom to know the difference.

This powerful prayer enabled me to find more inner strength and healing each and every day. Try it for yourself.

Good luck!

3 Exercises to Practice When Facing Loss

1. There are seven major energy centers in the body called Chakras.

These energy centers help you to maintain balance and flow within the body. It's like tuning a piano. If one note is off key, the piano is not 100 percent in full functionality.

Similar to the body, if one, two, or even all of these energy centers are not functioning properly, gradually the body starts to feel dis- (meaning NOT) ease or "disease." Therefore it is crucial to (ideally) maintain and balance the chakras on a daily basis.

The seventh chakra is located on top of your head. It is known as the Crown chakra. The color associated with the seventh chakra is white or violet. This color is connected to the Higher Power, Source, God (whatever label you call it). The seed sound for this chakra is "*Om.*"

Repeat this mantra as many times as you wish. It's a wonderful way to get out of your head and into your heart and connect with the almighty power.

2. Write down at least five things you *can do.* It will motivate you to believe and be a better version of yourself.

While facing loss it's easy to downfall into the "I can't, I am blocked, I won't" mode. Shift it around and focus on your abilities and what you CAN DO in the Now.

3. Be out in nature.

Nature is an incredible resource and a beautiful reminder of the ebb and flow of life. We create, sustain, and lose in nature just as much as in life itself.

Being outdoors enables you to put things into perspective. There are four seasons within the year which intermittently change year after year. As humans, we cannot ignore the notion of loss, similarly to being entrenched within Mother Nature's fluctuating weather patterns. We cannot ignore nature's way either.

Soak up nature's ancient wisdom by enjoying a stream, lake, river, or ocean. Take a hike through the wilderness, or just sit next to the trunk of a tree. This enables one to raise your vibration with what is, as is, with no wishful thinking, just being.

The best part of nature is not only do you feel fresh and alive, nature is free and accessible for everyone.

Coloring Outside
the Lines

When I was a young schoolgirl in kindergarten, back in the late '70s, the girls and boys teased me a majority of the time. That being said, I automatically felt that nobody was inclined to play or interact with me. Maybe this was because I was the one and only Indian little girl in the entire class and viewed as "different" in a predominantly Caucasian school district.

I was also the only five-year-old who had thick, rope-like braids in my hair and wore coke-bottle glasses to see better. Although I didn't think wearing glasses at such a tender age was such a big deal, my classmates did, calling me "four eyes."

The best feature of wearing glasses was that the frame was my favorite color: purple, a deep violet to be exact, with dusty rose and lavender flowers nestled on the rims of the frames. I was one of those girls who would rather make a mess, play hopscotch, and climb trees than be bound by four walls in kindergarten class.

Throughout my childhood, I was in complete nirvana land when I played with colors. My favorite playtime toy was Light-Bright, where I would create my own masterpiece using an array of rainbow-colored pegs that lit up when you plugged it into an outlet. Furthermore, I loved going to art class in particular, crafting with something tangible like clay. I was on cloud nine getting down and dirty with that glop of thunderstorm-color clay the size of my fist. Anything and everything that involved using my hands while being highly imaginative enlightened my heart and soul.

I might have only been five tears young, but I always knew I was an "old soul." My free-spirited passion for life was at odds with kindergarten class, which was inundated with strict rules and regulations. I also was considered a "slow learner" because I didn't learn the alphabet and numbers as fast as the other kids. As a result, I always felt like an outcast.

To top it all off, my teacher, Mrs. Newton, made my kindergarten days torturous, which didn't help me build any self-esteem. All the little girls and boys adored the teacher, except me. I sensed that she was somewhat shrewd with her rock-hard, controlling behavior.

She appeared to be too perfect and looked like she had a brand-new haircut and style every single day of class. I intuitively sensed her authoritative ways toward teaching and just looking at her made me feel like wetting my pants. Her superficial smile added more agony to my five-year-old self. I constantly struggled trying to catch up with my classmates in topics that disinterested me. In addition, behind Mrs. Newton's snow-white teeth I sensed judgment, especially toward me.

I know I was a little weird and extremely sensitive.

However, I just wanted to "be seen" and accepted by my fellow peers. The catty, chatty girls purposely excluded me by creating their own Girl-Power tag-team. In particular, there was a blonde girl named

Jenna and a redhead named Beth. They dominated all of us kids (especially the girls) and had their own private section on the jungle gym.

During recess, these girls were always on the top of the dome doing crazy flips and hanging upside down. It was as if they could do no wrong because they were the popular kids and demanded attention from everybody else.

In retrospect, I was always more introverted than extroverted. And recess never felt like an uplifting experience. As a result, I would get bored after only ten minutes. Eventually I found it too hard and overbearing trying to break open and be a part of the girls' group. So I didn't waste any more of my time after awhile.

The boys were typical five-year-olds and didn't like to play with me because I was a girl and had the cooties (otherwise known as "girl germs").

One day, Mrs. Newton allowed the class to color for a short period. I was sitting at a triangle-shaped table next to Jason and Otis. These were the only boys who would occasionally include me during recess while playing freeze-tag, bouncing off the monkey bars, or just skipping around on the playground. Jason and Otis felt safe for me because they didn't attach themselves to any specific clique or group.

During coloring time, Mrs. Newton specifically directed us to use as many colors as we wished. However, there was only one rule to abide, and that was to color inside the lines. Almost immediately, I tuned out Mrs. Newton's instructions and grabbed that crimson-red crayon and colored away. I almost broke the crayon in two with my tight grip. With intense fire and passion, I naturally colored outside the lines. It was my time to go wild and crazy with color and I was unstoppable.

Meanwhile, Otis and Jason snickered at me. I ignored them until Otis exclaimed: "Amla, you're coloring outside the lines!"

"Yes, I am!" I shouted defiantly.

To make matters worse, Jason sneered at me as if I had stolen his lunch money. Otis and Jason then threatened my inner peace by raising their hands and yelling, "Teacher, teacher, Amla colored outside the lines!"

"Go ahead, tell the teacher!" I exclaimed. I didn't care because it was my "Amla time" to color away as if I was holding the last crayon on earth.

Mrs. Newton hurried over to my table and looked at me with her stone-cold eyes.

"Why did you color outside the lines Amla, when I told you not to?" she sharply asked. She scolded me like I was a little stray dog, all alone and fending for myself.

I looked up with my big, doe-like eyes and said, "Because I wanted to, and I love coloring, Mrs. Newton."

"If you cannot follow the rules, you cannot go to recess as your punishment!" she snapped in response.

As Mrs. Newton continued to hover, I sunk deeper and deeper into my chair, hunched over like a ninety-five-year-old grandma. It humiliated me because the entire class watched and overheard Mrs. Newton reprimand me for me coloring outside the lines. For the first time in my short five years of life, I felt as if I'd been sucker-punched in the stomach. All because I had bent the rules, followed my heart, and colored outside the lines.

Mrs. Newton stared down at the halfway-colored picture I was working on. I gulped down as my throat caved in. I fought the tears from falling down my disgruntled face. I could sense Otis and Jason gawking at me, but they didn't utter a word. And it didn't matter anyway because they knew I was under scrutiny.

I wondered what I had done so awfully wrong that Mrs. Newton felt compelled to make a prime example of me as I was the epitome example of a mistake for the kindergarten class to learn from.

Why was she so critical of me? Just because I chose to listen to my heart's desires and needs instead of obeying her rules?

After a few minutes, the bell rang for recess. I quickly slid out of my chair and lined up by the door with the other kids. I had hoped that Mrs. Newton would somehow "forget" that she had forbade me from going to recess as my punishment. Unfortunately, that was my own wishful thinking.

"No, not you, Amla," said Mrs. Newton, pointing her finger at me. "Go back to your desk and put your head down; you're not going outside to play today."

I walked back to my desk wearing a huge frown on my face. I held back my tears as I heard my classmates march out of Mrs. Newton's classroom. Their chirpy voices became fainter and more distant until I heard nothing. Meanwhile, the ghost-town classroom I occupied was pin-drop silent, and this scared me.

Mrs. Newton kept an eye on me. I distinctly remember her touching the top of my head with her sticky-hot hands, making sure my head stayed down during the entire time of recess.

From that day forward, I questioned and second-guessed my true heart's desires. Because I thought that if I honored them, I'd somehow be punished for my "bad behavior."

Due to that specific kindergarten incident, I never felt confident enough to trust my gut instincts versus abiding by the rules and regulations dictated by my teacher (or anybody else, for that matter).

As an adult, I still feel the need to listen to and oblige other people's expectations of how I should exude my behavior and actions. Especially while interacting with any authority figures.

As a result, I always felt "less capable" while growing up, and I developed low self-esteem. More so, I never exuded any self-respect for myself, because I didn't know that it existed in the first place.

With that, I genuinely believed that the initial answers for true happiness were external versus internal. And these belief systems, positive or negative, uprooted from that subconscious "start point" in Mrs. Newton's Kindergarten class. Needless to say, kids are taught the good, bad, and in-between when people model through their actions, not their words. With that, I inadvertently endured mixed messages and was consistently tested by my outside circumstances on when to follow the rules and when to trust and follow my heart.

I will never forget my sweet soul friend, Kalpen, a boy I met as a teen back in 1990. There was something intriguing about him when we initially met in New Jersey at an Indian camp. I first noticed Kalpen in the dining hall where all the campers and volunteers gathered for dinner.

I absolutely loved his original style; he looked like a hippie with his shoulder-length wavy hair, wearing a psychedelic mustard, orange, and caramel-color tie-dyed T-shirt. No doubt, I was magnetically drawn to hang out with him from day one at camp.

Indian camp (for Indians born, raised, or inherited India traits) was a perfect fit for kids like Kalpen and me because we were both first generation, born and raised in the United States. More importantly,

Kalpen and I established a hungry desire to dabble and learn more about our traditional Indian heritage.

At this camp we experienced our culture through morning meditation and yoga. After all, yoga originated in India over 500 years ago. And even though Kalpen and I found yoga a bit dry, we knew it was beneficial for our health, not only physically, but more so spirituality, for our hearts and souls. As a result, every day at camp we got up around 7:00 a.m., threw on some sweatpants and a T-shirt, and headed out to yoga for an hour session.

Indian camp also included Indian games like cricket and something called "steal the bacon," although our camp faculty and volunteers (who we called aunties and uncles) refused to use this specific title because we were Hindus. As Gandhi once said, "We believe in nonviolence." Therefore, all of us campers and volunteers ate vegetarian meals throughout the week. I had no problem with that because I had been raised vegetarian since early childhood.

There were also outdoor activities like canoeing and kayaking and, of course, what's a camp without an actual campfire?

One of my favorite features of attending Indian camp was snacking on s'mores made with marshmallow, chocolate, and graham crackers. And the added bonus experience was when we gathered around the campfire, this one guy would play his acoustic guitar and strum to the song "More Than Words." That was my all-time favorite song back in the day, and the greatest hit of 1990.

I was sixteen then, and Kalpen was a couple years younger. At camp we were always in our own little world, chatting up deep conversations about how we would never take life for granted.

I admired Kalpen's mixed-blend personality of passion along

with a wild-side twist. He was definitely a non-conformist, and maybe that's exactly why I was so tuned into him. We were like two peas in a pod because we didn't conform and try to fit in with most people.

At first I wasn't aware, until Kalpen mentioned that he liked me. I was clueless because I was crushing on another guy at camp, named Hem. In fact, Kalpen and I struck up our first conversation because I liked Hem; I sat beside both of them after dinner while waiting for the Indian cultural program to begin.

In hindsight, it was quite flattering that Kalpen liked me just a little bit. However, our friendship blossomed into something more wholesome and solid; we were good friends, and I was thrilled to call him my go-to guy. Kalpen and I clicked like turning on a light switch. And he always made me smile no matter how my days were spent: happy, sad, or in between.

He was the nutty peanut butter and I was the fruity grape jelly; together, we made a great sandwich combination.

After camp ended, we continued our beautiful bond and exchanged insightful ideas with one another. These were the days when long-distance calls were quite expensive using landlines (our only option). Nevertheless, we spiked up our parents' phone bills and easily talked for a couple hours every week (me living in Connecticut and him living in Massachusetts).

Kalpen and I shared some incredibly inspiring stories, even in our most vulnerable teenage years. One day, I sharply remember him asking me, "Amla, if you knew you were going to die tomorrow, what would you do?"

I paused for a few moments and said I would pray to God and

ask for forgiveness if I had committed any sins in my sixteen years of life as Amla.

"Amla, you're going to die tomorrow and you're worried about your sins? Really?" This revved Kalpen up, so I reversed the question.

"Kalpen, what would you do if you were to die tomorrow?" I asked.

"I'd rob a bank; I'd speed down the highway at one hundred miles an hour. Basically, I would do anything and everything outside of my moral code of conduct," he boldly said.

I was stunned to hear his words. "Why? Why would you do that?" I asked with concern.

He sighed. "Amla, if I'm going to die tomorrow, who cares about the consequences? I gotta go out and live without any fear, including my last day on earth," he exclaimed.

He had a thought-provoking point. Immediately after that particular call, I played our conversation like a broken record in my head. Maybe I was more tarnished than I thought with Mrs. Newton's conditioned behavior impacting me as a teenager. Therefore, at this stage of my life, I believed in following my own morals and values rather than breaking the rules.

I believe Karma follows you everywhere, just like your shadow. Eventually, you will face the consequences of your decisions and actions whether it's in this lifetime or not. Lucky for me, as a camper, I read several Indian comic books that offered a great resource of tales and stories based on Karma.

Interestingly enough, I had discovered and found out about Gyrate Atrophy in April of 1990, and that summer, in August,

Kalpen and I first met. And even though Kalpen knew about my eye condition, he accepted me in totality.

Kalpen was a gifted and intelligent young man. During his high school years, he attended a local college part-time. No doubt, he was one of those kids who never had to work conscientiously in school.

Meanwhile, I was challenged academically throughout my school years. I would work diligently on each and every subject just to get solid grades like As and Bs. More Bs to be honest.

One summer, Kalpen was returning back home from a baseball game. He sat in the front passenger side of the car. The vehicle he occupied passed through a yellow blinking light and crossed an intersection.

Suddenly, a drunk driver collided into the car directly into Kalpen's passenger-side door—the only part of the car that was crushed. This tragic accident knocked him unconscious and he was in a coma for approximately one year. Sadly, my near and dear friend Kalpen, passed away in 1993.

His sister, Ushma, called me from Newton, Massachusetts, to deliver this devastating news. My heart shattered into a million pieces and Kalpen's loss intrinsically affected me. I was in such disbelief. I held the phone in mid-air, listening to the non-stop beeping noise that indicated the other party had hung up the phone but I had not.

I stared at the phone for hours, shocked, faking myself out, thinking this was all just hocus-pocus and Kalpen would call me a day or two later. I couldn't believe the best friend I had ever known and purely loved was gone. Gone.

Why? WHY, God? How can you steal him away from his loved

ones and me? What am I going to do without you, Kalpen? You were my best friend, and God basically said your time is up! WHY?

I mourned Kalpen for months and years on end. Only through time did my grief and sorrow transform into a huge appreciation for his brief physical presence in my life. Kalpen's amazing insight and his wise, food-for-thought ways of living will forever be embedded within my brain.

After he died, I reflected on our intense conversation when he'd asked me, "Amla, what would you do if you knew you were going to die tomorrow?" The irony? He's the one who died a few years later.

Kalpen was the one who inspired me to live without being consumed by other people's judgment or actions. He was the one who reinforced that it was perfectly okay NOT to follow the rules. Inferring that it's perfectly okay to color outside the lines (no pun intended). And the most profound lesson I've learned due to Kalpen's passing at such a tender age is that life is way too short and to LIVE life. Meaning, don't watch your life skate on by. Nevertheless, taking risks is a huge factor in life, and I should embrace and expect the unexpected because nothing in life is a slam-dunk guarantee. Kalpen's persona and spirit influenced me to be the best version of me by being brave and taking giant leaps of faith in life, despite the outcome.

There are consequences and repercussions for every action one takes. However, that doesn't mean you cannot allow yourself to frolic beyond the limits of your personal comfort zone. And a comfort zone is just that: comfortable, secure, and safe.

Almost every action you choose while stepping up the ladder of life involves taking a risk. This is especially true when fueling your heart and soul. In the end, whether you venture out on the wild side and color outside the lines or choose not to, it's all about finding balance and encompassing the yin and yang of life.

You can only balance your right brain (creative side) with your left brain (logical side) hemispheres by giving yourself permission to fail, a chance to make mistakes. Either your individual decisions run parallel and follow the rules or they do not. After all, we're human beings, and mistakes are inevitable.

Furthermore, there is a time to contemplate and make practical decisions, and there are times when you are submerged into the deep waves of life. That being said, life involves the heads and tails of a coin: risk-taking and practicality. It's not either/or, it's both.

It's perfectly okay to break the rules from time to time because, if you don't, you'll never know how far you can excel from the mind, body, and spirit. For instance, if one doesn't take risks here or there, one cannot find true love, move to a new city, or even drive a car.

On the flip side, if you never obey any rules or regulations (like making a complete stop at a stop sign intersection or paying your taxes) there would be complete chaos and no order in the world. The priceless question is: when do you passionately "take that chance" and when do you stand back, follow through mechanically, and stick with the rules?

It can be a tricky decision as an adult. There is nobody standing next to you 24 hours a day to set forth guidelines and enforce personal boundaries. You are the master of your own life by using discernment and what works for your individual needs. More importantly, there is no life manual on how to live your life. However, you do the best you can, with the cards you are dealt, just like in poker. Whether you have a good hand or a bad hand, you make a "play" with the cards that are dealt for you—not anybody else's cards. Ultimately, Kalpen taught me how to live a meaningful and fruitful life without any regret, vision or no vision. And I am forever grateful for my kindred spirit connection with Kalpen.

Life is literally a "trip." So enjoy the ride, fast or slow, turbulent or smooth. More importantly, when you decide to color outside the lines, no matter what, it's worth taking the chance. After all, a life is not a life if you just exist. A life is a true life when you fully LIVE.

3 Exercises that Empower
You to Take That Chance and Fulfill Great
Opportunities

1. Use discernment.

Ask yourself this significant question while placing your hand on your heart: if I choose A, B, C situation, will this serve my highest and holiest good?

Remember that taking chances is never about serving your immediate wants and needs like a kid crying for candy. Taking a chance, metaphorically speaking, is about using mindfulness and looking both ways before you cross the street, so to speak. Your heart knows what to do. Use it as your GPS navigation system, guiding you to your final destination.

2. The third chakra (energy center) is connected to the color sunshine yellow.

As previously mentioned (chapter one exercises), there are seven main energy centers that enable you to preserve equilibrium within the body. Chakra three is located just above your navel (the Solar Plexus area). The color associated with this chakra is "sunshine yellow."

The seed sound connected with chakra three is "*Ram.*" Feel free to repeat this mantra along with imagining the bright color yellow. By doing so, it allows you to obtain self-confidence, will-power, and honor your own strength.

3. Positive affirmations.
1. I stand tall in order to be my ALL.
2. I am capable, confident, and strong.
3. I can manifest anything my heart desires because I am limitless.

Repeat these affirmations as many times as you wish.

Good luck!

Finding Courage Through Change

It was 1999 and I was working at the Hartford Life Insurance Company in Simsbury, Connecticut. I was doing very well, gradually climbing up the success ladder, working within the Human Resources Department. I had an entry-level position, with great aspirations to become one of the best head recruiters for this company. I knew I would be an exceptional asset for the team because I love helping people. And nothing beats the feeling of seeing the priceless expression on a person's face when they are offered their ultimate dream job.

One day, my boss asked me to substitute for a colleague, answering phone calls from potential recruits. Due to the unexpected overflow of calls, I scrambled around placing people on hold, or the incoming phone calls would go straight into voicemail. And when the person left a message, a blinking red light would flash on the console. Although, for some reason, I had difficulty seeing the light. In addition, the light appeared faded while I experienced double vision.

Right then, a gentle voice said, *Something might be wrong with your eyesight, Amla!*

And instead of listening to my instincts, I ignored them. The stakes were too high for the possibility of a significant decline in my eyesight. And to make matters worse, the slight chance of any more vision loss would diminish my efficiency and raise concern pertaining to my proficiency level at a job I valued each and every day.

One month later, I woke up literally seeing blobs. I peered outside my bedroom window and couldn't identify any tree branches in my backyard. The new way I was seeing reminded me of seventh grade science class; it was like trying to identify an amoeba underneath the microscope. Everything appeared as a big blur; shapeless, distorted, and pale. I screamed at the top of my lungs, "No, this cannot be happening to me!"

What about my dream job as a recruiter? How am I to make a well-established career for myself if I cannot see? The prognosis for complete blindness is supposedly between ages forty-five and sixty. I'm twenty-five years old and way too young to be sightless right now!

I wanted answers pronto.

After multiple calls to Dr. Kaiser's office at NIH, I finally had my chance to consult with an on-call technician. She treated me as if I were a specimen to be examined by a physicist. As my voice quivered through the frequency of the telephone, I aggressively asked her why I was seeing physical blobs of "nothingness."

In a flat monotone voice she responded, "Well, it's most likely that you have developed cataracts due to your eye condition, Gyrate Atrophy. I suggest you go to your local ophthalmologist to confirm my hypothesis."

"Fine," I said, and we both hung up.

Call me neurotic, but I assumed that Dr. Kaiser would've

warned me that cataracts in my twenties is "normal" for patients like me experiencing gradual vision loss. However, she didn't as my primary ophthalmologist, and I was ticked off.

I felt handcuffed and helpless. Me, "suddenly" seeing unidentifiable objects on top of enduring tunnel vision leading into blindness. I was outraged and questioned how much more turmoil I would tolerate in this lifetime.

I contacted a top-notch cataract eye specialist named Dr. Gilbert and scheduled an appointment in March of 1999. Once again, I was off to see another ophthalmologist in the midst of chaos, conflict, and confusion.

During my tedious eye exam, Dr. Gilbert verified that I had developed cataracts and said that he would be willing to perform the surgery to remove the "dirty lens." I instantly froze because that same year, our family friends' grandmother developed cataracts, had eye surgery, and due to unforeseen circumstances after the operation, she went blind in one eye.

No fail, I was freaked out.

This was all so surreal. How would I tackle and push through this massive roadblock?

Most twenty-somethings are invested in building a solid career, hanging out socially, and aspiring to make a stable and independent life for themselves. And then there's me. Within the past decade, I'd been diagnosed with a debilitating eye disease. I received and lost my driver's license within four years, in addition to losing a valuable piece of my independence after being declared legally blind. I then lost my grandmother, and now I am caught in between another crossfire, facing cataracts—all at the whopping age of twenty-five.

What's next, giving up my arm and a leg? Why is my life so satu-rated with such extreme forms of inexplicable change?

As a result, even though I was panicky and reluctant about un-dergoing cataract surgery, my sense of practicality surfaced up to go through with it despite the fact that within the bigger picture I was still living with Gyrate Atrophy.

The day of my surgery will be imprinted in my brain for the rest of my life. I was a basket case as my mom and I drove closer and clos-er to the Hartford hospital. I was on pins and needles and wondered how I would survive another unexpected change, knowing that there might be a small chance of complications after surgery. Although, as Dr. Gilbert reassured me at my initial eye consultation, "Amla, it's very rare that any negative results occur after cataract surgery."

When we arrived at the outpatient check-in area, the reception-ist instructed me to change into a hospital gown in order to prep for surgery. Next, the anesthesiologist entered my outpatient room.

"Please give me a minimum dosage of anesthesia, because I am highly sensitive," I pleaded.

She complied, and I assumed she had injected a low dosage.

Prior to the start of surgery, I vaguely recall drifting in and out of consciousness, feeling weak and vulnerable as I lay flat on my back on the table in the operating room.

Dr. Gilbert then leaned in and whispered into my ear, "Okay, Amla. I'm going to begin the procedure."

And because I'd received such a mild dosage of anesthesia, my body jolted up and formed an "L" shape on the table. I barely heard Dr. Gilbert command a nurse to administer a higher dose of anes-thesia, and only then was I OUT like a light.

After surgery, as I was being wheeled out of the operating room, almost immediately, I sobbed away.

The concerned female nurse asked, "Why are you crying?"

Fighting to hold back my tears from cascading down my face, I exclaimed, "I don't want to go blind!"

When I had fully awakened from recovery, my mom was there to greet me with her heart-warming smile. And that's all I needed to melt away all of my troubles for that day. My mom was my number-one fan, a superior supporter of me until this day, and she always will be.

Two weeks after I'd recovered from surgery, I was seeing lopsided because my right eye had been "fixed" while my left eye was substantially compromised. As a result, I had no choice but to quit my job at the Hartford life insurance company. I was oblivious to how empty I would feel until after I called my boss to inform her the grim news.

"Oh, Amla, I am so sorry to hear about this. I wish you only the best, and good luck in your next chapter in life," she compassionately responded.

I wished all of my ophthalmologists emulated similar empathy illustrated by my now former boss.

Within the blink of an eye, I transitioned from a dedicated career woman moving my way up to success, to a scattered and displaced legally blind lady. As a result, I was both the host and the singular guest at my own "pity party."

The majority of people like me with normal vision physically healing from cataract surgery experience crystal-clear vision shortly after the recovery period. On the contrary, people living with Gyrate Atrophy like myself experience sharper vision for a brief number of years after surgery. However, over time, the vision subsides, losing its sharpness, its brightness in distinguishing color, and ultimately worsens. As a result, I had undergone both cataract surgeries by 2001.

After the initial aftermath of my first cataract surgery, my eyes were figuratively wide open. Meaning, it was as if I had been reborn all over again, and my heart expanded and opened up into being vulnerable whenever, with whomever. A perfect example of this was when the nurse was extremely unaware that I was going blind. I didn't care who was listening. I merely needed to blurt out the disheartening news for me, myself, in order to validate this traumatic change in my life. And by bravely unleashing my exposed vulnerability immediately after surgery, I was clearly on the road to healing and recovery by adapting and learning to accept change.

Years later, I had an epiphany moment and realized that almost every aspect of my life revolves and evolves around my vision loss.

Everything, including career, relationships, being physically mobile (simply moving from one side of the room to the other), being self-sufficient—heck, even brushing my teeth—will be more tedious and time consuming without any vision.

Undesirable change is never easy, but it's necessary for the nub of the soul to evolve, transmute, and ascend throughout life.

Before cataract surgery, I had only experienced nearsighted vision. Post-surgery, I maintained nearsighted vision by wearing reading glasses. On a positive note, my distance vision increased significantly. So I was content for a few years of seeing like I was watching a cartoon on television, with the brilliant colors of the characters jumping off the television screen. Overall, I was amazed at how crisply I could see.

Needless to say, by facing Gyrate Atrophy, I encountered way too many changes, much too rapidly for my "Amla livelihood." I felt like I was going through puberty all over again, over-exaggerated, awkward change, and just when I was adapting to a new reality, the universe threw out another pop test.

Unfortunately, three or four years after both cataract surgeries, my eyesight faded away and I never saw simple food the same way again. My vision had degraded to the point where I was no longer able to distinguish between the individual grains of rice on my dinner plate, which looked more like mashed potatoes.

Cataracts also desensitized my ability to enjoy colors. For instance, my "new way" of seeing was like buying a brand new magenta T-shirt. The new shirt is fresh and vibrant in color. But, after a few washing machine cycles and throwing it into the dryer, the fabric fades and the T-shirt loses its brilliance in color. This is a perfect example of the way I currently see all colors: dull and smoky in texture.

I felt depleted with no clue as to how to live a purposeful life for the rest of my life.

Within a few months I surrendered and succumbed to managing my parents' business. It was my only way of feeling empowered. I was always savvy at sales and had often worked at the store during my teenage years. I took charge of sales, bought merchandise for the store, created an e-commerce website, which led me to managing our retail store.

We sold tapestries, hippy-dippy clothes, and home decor products that infused an East-meets-West flavor. However, within five to ten years, I felt stuck in the mud, like there was more to life than just selling stuff. With that, I had a "spiritual awakening" and felt the need to feed and nourish my heart's desires.

I attempted to move on by being patient and compassionate towards myself. However, my life was in shambles because I felt isolated from any human contact. I even distanced myself from my family as a form of my own armor and protection to maneuver through these tough times.

How can I console my family if I can't help myself?

Interestingly enough, when there was downtime at the store, I naturally started writing. Since I was a teenager, I'd enjoyed expressing myself through journaling. And when I was diagnosed with Gyrate Atrophy, I would spend hours upon hours writing in my notebook as a healthy outlet into the wee hours of the night.

Nevertheless, I felt so liberated when the pen was in my hand. I knew I had proficient skills as a writer, which were heightened and enhanced during my college years. (This was predominantly because all of my final exams consisted of submitting twenty-page papers.)

Without any doubt, writing was not only uplifting, it was effortless; I was doing something truly fulfilling that didn't involve struggle. And just like that, my true purpose was born.

Of course, I've learned some valuable lessons as a result of these life-changing circumstances. Experiencing unexpected change makes most people feel uncomfortable. That is, within my personal life, every time my vision changes, I'm kicked out of my comfort zone. Therefore, I had no choice but to get comfortable being uncomfortable.

The most agonizing aspect of going through unexpected change is the not-so-subtle feeling of moving two steps forward and three steps back. Gradually losing my vision poisoned my sense of motivation and drive, especially right after both cataract surgeries.

The truth is that nothing in our lives is consistent, and that's one of the most fearful factors of encountering surprise change. In a nutshell, the only thing that is consistent is the notion of inconsistency.

Being human, my mind fluctuated back and forth like the ball in a ping-pong match. I habitually contemplated my future endeavors and what they might entail, when and if, I was sightless.

And, because I was literally in between stages of physically seeing and not seeing intermittently, I learned to adapt and practice the art of being detached, especially pertaining to the short-lived and fast-moving physical changes with my eyesight.

Gradually going blind has gradually taught me a long lasting lesson: that everything is temporary. Everything, including my own heartbeat, which never beats or vibrates at the same frequency.

If this takes place internally, why wouldn't it happen externally?

Hands down, change can be extremely difficult because it is human nature to fear the unknown and easily get attached to expectations, especially when immersed in unpredictable experiences.

Prior to discovering that I had developed cataracts, I genuinely believed my life was on the verge of making insurmountable leaps and bounds, leading into astronomical career success.

However, the universe choreographed another plan. I merely hadn't recognized the blessings by facing these life-long lessons.

In retrospect, I realize that change is inevitable and a force to be reckoned with. Nonetheless, I had the choice to linger in my own self-inflicted pity, or NOT.

Only with time and space have I learned to honor my authentic emotions in order to move forward one step at a time. And every so often I literally stumble because I'm subjected to living with less vision.

More importantly, by enduring cataracts, I had no choice but to let go of ego and the need to control how and when things happen. As humans, we want things our way, right away. However, I genuinely believe there is a divine plan for each and every one of us.

The only thing we can control is how we, as human beings, respond through the ebb and flow of life. Gyrate Atrophy has been a phenomenal teacher in showing me how to live in the moment, because every moment is multifaceted and changeable at the snap of two fingers.

Occasionally, as humans, we might push down hard, pumping the brakes when we encounter unexpected change; however, major change and growth spurts most commonly occur through pain and suffering. The thought-provoking question is: how does one naturally move through the change (positive or negative)?

All organisms grow and flourish within their own organic time and space. As a result, there is no one-size-fits-all pertaining to how people could or should evolve.

A simple example: Just because two people are of the same age, gender, or ethnicity, doesn't mean they are experiencing the exact same life-altering lessons along the path of life. Therefore, each and every one of us learns and grows through change in numerous and widespread directions. And that's exactly what makes this world so enriched with such beauty.

When encountering change, you must rearrange and reflect upon the specific situation naturally through time. Just like in nature, every autumn the leaves on trees turn vibrant colors of golden yellow, to orange, to burnt orange, to rust red to brown. Eventually, all the leaves break off, dancing and drifting through the nippy fall temperatures, finally falling down to the ground. Nature has its unique way of sifting through change, not against it, as I have proactively learned on the journey of gradually losing my vision.

The key factor to remember while experiencing the change is "allowing." Slow yourself down and pause through change. Only then can you make wiser and more effective decisions regarding moving through the change. And when in doubt, stand still and just breathe. Because, in the end, it takes patience, patience, and more patience to recover and heal through any change.

I have discovered there are three main ingredients to thrive and survive through any type of change:

1) Feel or absorb the change. That is, allow the unwanted feeling of change to penetrate your heart. When you feel your emotions (positive or negative), you prevent yourself from any further suppression that may lead to resentment. (Trust me, I've experienced this too.) You must feel in order to truly heal. After all, "e-motions" are just that, "energy in motion," which represents impermanence.

Eventually, the emotions will lose their potency if one chooses to face them directly from the root (again, feeling your feelings because this too, shall pass). With that, do not overly consume yourself with the emotions. An important disclaimer: this does not mean that you allow temper tantrums anywhere you physically are as an adult because "you feel" the emotions. Be mindful and vigilant to feel your emotions within a safe and protected environment in order to honor your authentic self.

More importantly, the positive and negative feelings are compulsory and symbolize a stepping-stone for personal growth, big or small. Think of a battery charging your remote control. You need a negative and positive charge of the battery to have a full-functioning device. Feelings are just that, feelings. Once you absorb them, positive or negative, the initial "power you may have fed" to your emotions tapers off and eventually dissolves away.

2) Digest the change. (This does not mean "swallowing the change," which many of us, including myself, naturally do because it's a quick and easy "fix.") The best way to get through any change is to allow it to percolate within YOU, in order to allow the change to permeate through YOU.

Furthermore, there isn't a "magic pill" antidote to push through the change, whether it be a bitter divorce, a geographic move because of a new job, or heartache over the death of a loved one. No matter how extreme the circumstances, sooner or later, one must allow his or her feelings to seep into their pure essence. It's never easy, but it's a healthy choice for healing and recovering through change.

3) Surrender. Surrender does not mean giving up and throwing your hands in the air. On the contrary, surrender means to trust yourself and detach from the outcome.

A beautiful example of surrendering is to imagine holding a helium balloon. If you clasp on too tightly, you're

preventing yourself from witnessing the infinite possibilities as the balloon rises and drifts up to the heavens.

However, if you simply let go and allow the balloon to carry
itself wherever the final destination may be, there is a subtle empowering feeling when you trust your gut and truly
believe that whatever is meant to be will be, and that everything happens for your soul's purpose. Just have faith!

Most importantly, out of all three crucial steps, you must master
step one, feeling the change, and two, digesting the change *prior* to
surrendering and letting go of the entire "in flux" experience. Bottom
line, one has to purely "want to let go" in order to sincerely surrender
the "knowingness" from the heart (faith and trust) versus the "knowingness" from the head (ego and control). There is a vast difference.

Trust me based on my personal hardcore experiences; if you
can view change as an adventure versus a mundane chore, your soul
will soar and gravitate toward liberation and limitless possibilities.
Essentially, becoming "friends" with the change enables you to realize that you can persevere through any challenge as long as you
know that people, places, things, and experiences are all just temporary. However, the spirit is not; it's everlasting and eternal.

Food for thought: As humans, the majority of us embrace
change when it's positive, but why is it so difficult to maneuver
through "speed bump" changes? My subjective answer: "positive
change is easy to accept" (like buying a car or home, finding a new
job, or going on vacation), while encountering negative change can
feel like rolling a boulder uphill. Life is full of changes big or small;
embrace it and move forward with grace. Good luck!

3 Exercises to Practice While Experiencing Change

1. The positive affirmation of "This too shall pass."
Just a friendly reminder: everything is temporary. Therefore, this is a simple yet effective way to move through change. Be present and repeat this affirmation as many times as you desire.

2. Meditate.
Learn to observe your breath by:

a) Closing your eyes.

b) Observing your inhale and exhale like viewing an ocean wave. Feeling the inhale coming in and the exhale going out.

c) Practice for at least five minutes and increase your time as you wish. It helps you anywhere and everywhere. After all, breath is life!

3. Sometimes, if you are stuck in the midst of change, you might want to seek professional help.
Whether it be through counseling or expressing yourself with a good friend, it's always beneficial to seek help, especially when unwanted change is upon your front doorstep.

Good luck!

Falling Hard
to Forgive

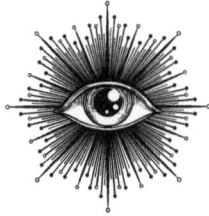

When I was a sophomore in high school, my older sister, Parul, commuted to and from the University of Connecticut. By the time I returned home from high school at approximately 2:30 p.m., she was already back home from her classes. Parul had two close-knit friends, Cindy and Sue, with whom she would yap away, either individually or with both of them simultaneously. That being said, she loved taking advantage of the new three-way calling feature on landlines back in the late '80s.

One time, being the annoying little sister I was, I overheard Parul talking to Sue, who mentioned that her older brother was interested in possibly dating her. Parul might have been playing it cool, but I was blown away. I couldn't believe the major changes occurring in my older sister's life, never mind her love life. When I would eavesdrop on her conversations, she waved her hands in my direction, shooing me away and shutting me out. Nevertheless, it was difficult maintaining privacy in our house, and of course, I didn't make Parul's life any easier by poking my nose into her fascinating life.

In comparison, my lack of a love life cornered me into becoming a late bloomer. Therefore, I didn't have my first kiss until I was twenty-one, which won the top award for being the worst kiss ever in my life.

The few men I found remotely interesting, or who were attracted to me, thought I was "too much." Goodness, even some of my girlfriends thought I was too much, forget potential boyfriends. As a result, I labeled myself as the "dumpee," who was almost always rejected by the potential suitor, which pierced my heart. That being said, you don't choose who you love; real love chooses you.

Furthermore, when I fall for somebody, I plunge in full force with everything I've got: all passionate, heart-expansive energy, with no walls blocking me. But that's what finding true love is all about, right? Falling face first, with no hesitation or armor deterring you away from the greatest love you could've possibly imagined for yourself.

Call me Cinderella, but I believe anything and everything is promising when it boils down to finding true love.

In the early fall of 2008, I was invited to a monthly meditation gathering. It was being held at an acquaintance's house, twenty minutes from my home. Finding a ride to and from this event posed as an obstacle, but I was optimistic I'd find one. I vaguely remembered the host, Michael, from another event that previous year.

The day of the gathering, I was apprehensive regarding attending the event altogether, although there was no valid reason why. I had a ride all set, a successful day running our family store, and my favorite part was the opportunity to engage with like-minded people and practice meditation.

What was the problem? I was the problem. I kept swaying back and forth, creating a whimsical "Amla dance" with myself. Once and for all, I whispered to the universe: "Should I go to this meditation?"

"Yes," a subtle voice replied. I surrendered, and I was on my way.

I was dropped off at an adorable little white house minutes away from my sister's college. After saying my goodbyes to my driver, I walked toward the house and found the garage door wide open, with strangers' shoes scattered by the entrance. After taking off my boots, I heard voices, but I didn't see anybody through the glass door so I knocked. Within seconds, a man slid across the floor on his stocking feet to greet me at the door.

"Are you Michael?" I asked.

"No, my name is Ed, but come on in. Welcome," he said.

"Thank you," I replied. I walked into the kitchen where a few people huddled around the warm stove drinking tea. Right then I glanced at Michael who was talking to another gentleman. I didn't want to disrupt them so I patiently waited to introduce myself. At last he took notice and approached me. "Hi, my name is Amla," I cheerfully said.

"I'm Michael. We previously talked over the phone," he said.

"Yes, yes," I replied. And to my surprise, just as I proceeded to shake his hand, Michael gave a gentle squeeze of my fingers and we hugged.

My heart skipped, literally. *What is happening*, I asked myself. I had never felt my heart jump-start like this in my whole thirty-four years of life.

This consumed me for a moment or two. However, I mechanically forced my mind to chime in because I wasn't in the privacy of my own space where I would have leisurely time to comprehend what had transpired. Maybe I didn't have to chew on anything because my heart showed me exactly what was going on. I was hooked on Michael. I merely didn't know how intense it was until that heartbeat of a moment.

At the gathering, Michael offered a video that featured a woman named Gangaji. All of her teachings, whether live or recorded, are based on different topics under the umbrella of spirituality.

During this particular orientation, via video, Gangaji mentioned that spirituality is everywhere, whether it be inside or outside closed doors. More importantly, spirituality is accessible for everyone, anywhere, at all times. She also stated that the spiritual practice generates from the heart, radiating unconditional love. However, in order for a person to integrate pure, unconditional love, the heart must break down to break open (Gangaji's most powerful message).

I found Gangaji's last main message most captivating: that even being a participant at discourses like this, or attending any other spiritual or holistic events, poses as an illusion and/or a distraction. Meaning, being on the spiritual path of enlightenment is solely an internal and independent work in progress FOR you, not something you do for or with others.

This profound message genuinely struck a chord within me and solidified my strong need to be an independent thinker and sustain individuality. *What an incredible and inspiring message Gangaji offered*, I thought to myself.

After the video presentation ended, Michael offered an informal group discussion. There were approximately ten people, some of whom snuggled together on the floor or on the L-shaped couch, while I chose to settle at the corner of the sofa with mismatched colorful pillows nestled on my lap. Michael sat by the television on a seat cushion, looking all cozy wrapped up in a warm blanket.

"Are there any questions or comments about this lecture?" Michael asked.

People raised their hands one by one and commented on Gangaji. I noticed how everyone was magnetically drawn toward Michael, and vice versa. He was an amazing facilitator and communicator when he interacted with the attendees. I was more reserved during the follow-up discussion but lightened up to some people as the night continued. And, because I depend on rides to and from places, I was the first person to leave. I waved goodbye to Michael, thanked him for the invite, and dashed out the door.

A week or two later I received a call from an unknown number on my flip phone. I glanced at it, wondering whether or not to answer, before I impulsively accepted the phone call.

"Hello?"

"Um, this is Michael, from the meditation gathering," he replied.

"Oh, hi, how are you?" I asked.

"Good," he replied.

He asked me my opinion of Gangaji's discourse, which led to several other miscellaneous spiritual topics before he suddenly changed the subject.

"Are you free on Friday? I won two tickets to the movies," he asked.

"Yes, sure. I'd love to go," I exclaimed.

"Great, I will pick you up at seven," he replied.

I gave him my address and we ended the call.

In retrospect, I genuinely believed that Michael and I were

going to the movies just as friends. And I was oblivious to the fact that an intelligent, gregarious, and spiritual guy like Michael, who just happened to be tall, dark, and handsome, would ever be interested in me. Nonetheless, after the movie, Michael drove me home, and we ended up having an in-depth philosophical conversation in my driveway. For once in my life, I felt confident and secure within my own skin.

From that day forward, we hit it off like nobody's business. Our feelings for one another blossomed effortlessly for approximately two months. We'd go out to spiritual gatherings within the community such as Kirtan (or Kirtana), a call-and-response musical event with the participants chanting out to the divine. We both loved taking brisk walks in nature, enjoyed teatime together, and even attended karaoke bars where we would sing our hearts away.

I admit, I was truly falling for Michael. We both had a similar outlook on life, with a complementary view of the world. And, to top it all off, he loved helping and serving the community just like me. (I get that quality from my mom. She volunteers and serves the seniors within our local community.)

By the end of November, Michael's tribe knew he and I were dating. He was involved in a variety of different social groups, whether it be through work, the local yoga center, or just being a dedicated participant within the holistic community. That being said, I only met a handful of people through Michael because he was quite the likable guy. Hands down, Michael was "Mr. Popular" within our local spiritual community, and I felt like an oddball standing beside Michael. This was all brand-new territory for me. And even though we'd already been dating a few months, I frequently questioned why

Michael was attracted to me, Amla, who'd been ignored and unseen most of my life.

My low self-esteem and inner self-critic cast a dark cloud over my head; I didn't believe I was worthy and deserving of being with Michael and placed him on a high pedestal. However, in spite of that itchy feeling, my heart continued to expand, and my sweet admiration for Michael blossomed naturally.

I never wanted to define or label our one-of-a-kind relationship because I was afraid I would jinx it. More so, I didn't want to lose Michael by projecting a "he is mine" attitude. And for the first time, I refused to portray myself as being "too much," like I was in my previous romantic relationships. All I desired was a deeply-connected, heartfelt, and loyal partnership with Michael.

One Saturday evening after another awesome date, Michael drove me home. And, as usual, when he parked the car in my driveway, we shared what felt like a forever hug. I argued with myself not to let him go, but it was past midnight.

As I tugged on the door handle to exit his car, I suddenly felt his hands gently caressing my back, doing the "spider dance," his fingers expanding and closing rhythmically. I was halfway out of the car and slipped back in. He caressed my hands and professed, "Amla, I love you!"

"Oh my God, I love you, too," I exclaimed. And within that split second, I realized I had loved Michael well before he declared those three words out loud.

I was stunned. Everything I imagined for myself with finding real, true love was coming into fruition. Michael loved me, Amla Mehta. We embraced one last time for the night, exchanged our goodbyes, and I headed into my house. As you might have guessed already, all night long, I was gushing. My entire body was tingling and zinging out of pure bliss.

"Wow, Michael said he loves me," I spoke aloud into the sweet darkness of my room. I was smitten with Michael's heartfelt declaration, and I repeated those words over and over all night long.

The next day, I couldn't stop smiling. This was my discreet little secret, tucked away in my heart, and I bathed myself in true happiness.

That same evening, Michael called me.

"How are you?" he asked.

"Fantastic, and you?"

"Amla, about last night…" He trailed off, and I knew something was wrong.

"You sound nervous," I said. "Is everything okay?"

"Amla, I am not in love with you. Did you feel my heart cringe when we hugged shortly after I expressed those three words?" he asked.

Huh? I questioned to myself. *How would I know your heart "cringed" after telling me you love me? I am not a heart reader.*

The remainder of the conversation felt like I was hearing Charlie Brown's teacher babbling on to the class, "wah, wah, wah." I was perplexed beyond words. *Who in their right mind does that? Michael downright expressed that he loves me and then snatches those words away not even twenty-four hours later. Why claim those words at all if he clearly didn't mean it?*

I wore my "Amla calm mask" through the remainder of that phone call, although I was utterly heartbroken to say the least.

In hindsight, I'm surprised I was disheartened for only a week or two following this particular conversation with Michael, considering the stakes of our relationship. However, my heart was hungry for Michael's love to intertwine with mine. Despite Michael stealing back those three life-changing words, I chose to continue our relationship.

In hindsight, I subconsciously pacified myself and believed that at least Michael was honest, and he revealed his genuine feelings almost immediately. More importantly, I thought if I gave Michael another chance, he might fall in love with me for real this time.

As a result, I allowed this scenario to slide down the chute and let it go. Thereafter, our relationship seemed to get back on track and most of our "dates" consisted of volunteering and serving at local homeless shelters.

In December 2008, my mom and I decided to visit our extended family in India. We bought airline tickets at the end of December and decided to depart from New York City at the end of January 2009.

Mom and I planned on visiting India for a total of five weeks. I was super excited because it had been seven years since I last visited India. My mom and I planned on visiting Bodh Gaya, located in eastern India, where Buddha received his enlightenment. I was ecstatic to experience this once-in-a-lifetime opportunity and visit Eastern India for the first time.

I acknowledged that spending five weeks and being 10,000 miles away from Michael would take a major toll on my heart. Therefore, I truly believed Michael was my everything.

When I informed Michael I planned on visiting India, he was extremely happy for me. And since there was a one-month gap between buying the airplane tickets and me departing for India, Michael and I continued to date, although it didn't feel enjoyable or full of compassion compared to the beginning of our blooming relationship.

Our true connection was on the fritz without any feel-good vibes. And yes, I know relationships shift and go through ups and downs. However, this stage of our relationship felt like a lost and empty life preserver floating in the middle of the ocean.

As the days zoomed by leading up to my departure for India, I could sense the depth of our relationship evaporating and feelings dispersing. I felt this way mainly because of one incident. In a nutshell, Michael hosted a potluck.

Right before dinnertime I asked, "Where are you sitting?"

He replied, "Amla, the table I'm at is full."

For God's sake, I am his girlfriend! I thought.

Michael didn't even insist on creating a spot for me. And because I was too busy volunteering, being the pseudo co-host at this gathering, everyone had already settled into their seats. This left me dining beside Michael's ex-girlfriend Jill at another table. Oh no, that wasn't kooky or uncomfortable.

On the heels of that particular gathering, something had splintered within Michael. And because of his passive aggressive behavior, he refused to unveil his internal feud with me. At first, I was intimidated to instigate "the talk." However, since we were already standing on the edge of our own cliff within the relationship, I initiated a meeting with Michael one last time before I left the country.

He picked me up from my house and we decided to go back to his place for dinner. Afterward, we plopped onto the couch to interact and discuss the loose outline of our relationship. I wasn't able to read his emotions. However, I chose to drive straight ahead with my true feelings.

"Michael, I feel like lately you have been acting very detached from me," I said.

He shrugged.

"And, because I am going to India for a lengthy amount of time, do you want to just go our separate ways? It might be for the best, considering I sense you are not invested in this relationship anymore," I said.

I had hand-delivered an easy-way-out pass to end the relationship. But to my surprise, he shook his head.

"No, no, no! Let's wait and see how things go. When you return from India we can meet in person and discuss our relationship in further detail," Michael said.

I hesitated, but then finally agreed with this unexpected proposition. Since he had reassured me that the relationship was not over, I clung for dear life to whatever the relationship title was between Michael and me.

I planned on calling Michael from India on a weekly basis to hear his voice for just a few minutes. (He had no idea I would do so either.) When I called every week, Michael was pleasant but implied he was too preoccupied almost every time. Our phone connections were staticky, and it felt like we were conversing under water. Ironically enough, this symbolized the status of our relationship: wavering and unclear.

By week three it was Valentine's Day, and I was feeling exhilarated at the thought of talking to Michael. When he answered the phone, he felt aloof and emotionally unavailable. I could sense he was dismissive and physically outside somewhere.

"Is this a good time?" I asked.

"I'm parking my car," he said.

I didn't allow myself to get all riled up because he was distracted, so I sweetly said, "Michael, happy Valentine's day!"

He didn't respond. Pause, space, nothing. He deflected, and mindlessly talked about other arbitrary topics before abruptly saying, "Listen, I gotta go. I am heading into a church right now."

I was dismayed and disappointed. I wasn't expecting a hearts-and-rainbows monologue describing his deep love for me, but saying "happy Valentine's day" in return would have been greatly appreciated. When we both hung up, my heart felt squashed down to the ground.

My eyes were wide open now, and I wholeheartedly knew our relationship had died.

How can Michael willingly elongate this relationship while I am 10,000 miles away, with no care in the world for my feelings?

Even after I had given him an easy opportunity to break up on the heels of leaving for India, Michael decided to hang on to our relationship by a thread. Nevertheless, Michael's actions were beyond disrespectful toward me.

The first Thursday in March 2009, I returned home from India. The next day, I set up a meeting with Michael at his rented massage studio. Based on Michael's previous behavior, I knew he would not take any responsibility to directly express that he wanted to end the relationship. But, I also knew somebody had to grab the bull by its horns and claim it, and that somebody happened to be me.

Essentially, I was cornered into doing the job "for him," which was mind-boggling, to say the least.

Despite feeling zonked from jet lag, the firecracker side of me needed to take charge. As I sat upright on his massage table, Michael purposely fled from any deep and meaningful conversations.

"Michael, when I was in India and I called you, I could sense you were distant and it was not because you and I were physically away from one another. You were point-blank distant," I said.

"Yes, Amla, I was, and I still am," he said.

"I guess it's really over between you and me. Isn't it?" I asked.

"Yes," he said.

He avoided any eye contact with me and remained silent after that last in-person confrontation. In my mind, not only was the relationship finally over; I felt somewhat relieved. Yet my heart felt charred, carving a deep and long-lasting "Michael scar" inside of my heart.

No fail, I fell hard for Michael. However, I fell harder for love! I spent the next few days recuperating from jet lag and sporadically regrouped from the Michael breakup. It was challenging; however, I was determined to push through the best way I could.

Exactly three weeks after the breakup, I received a voicemail from Michael asking me to return his phone call. His voice sounded unsettled yet eager to speak with me. Yes, I must confess, there was a huge part of me that yearned for Michael and I to "fight for us" and get back together. I impulsively called him back.

"Hi, Michael," I said.

He sighed. "Yes, Amla, I originally called to tell you something really important."

My heart thumped like I was at a drumming circle gathering.

"In order to prevent rumors, I wanted to tell you, firsthand, that I'm dating someone."

I couldn't believe my ears. Michael called to confess this late-breaking news. After a moment or two, I finally had the courage to speak up.

"So, who is it? Who are you dating?" I anxiously asked.

He hesitated for a moment and nonchalantly said, "Oh, it's Jill."

"What Jill?" I asked.

Jill was Michael's ex-girlfriend, now girlfriend? The woman I was stuck sitting next to at Michael's potluck dinner. Furthermore, this would be Michael's third time dating her.

Yes, it was "that Jill," and all I could do was shake my head in complete denial the entire time Michael was speaking.

I superficially replied, "Good for you, Michael. Good luck to you."

"I knew you would take this in stride, Amla. Thank you," he answered.

After I hung up the phone, I fought hard not to yell. *Why would Michael call me to claim he's dating somebody else? And out of all people, that somebody is Jill… Again!*

He didn't owe me any explanation; we were done.

Are we in high school all over again?

"In order to prevent rumors…" he said.

Oh, should I give Michael five gold stars because he performed a noble deed by sharing the current status of his love life?

Hypothetically speaking, what if I had discovered this "exciting news" from other people aside from Michael? If this ground-breaking news was 100 percent true, and it was, why would Michael suddenly be overly concerned about my feelings? Frankly speaking, Michael's current love life is none of my business.

I had dated a guy named Willy for five months until I broke up with him three weeks prior to dating Michael. Did I call Willy and tell him I was dating Michael?

No. I knew it might break Willy's heart. And, if Willy found out through other people, I had no control over other people's actions; I only had control over mine. I was shocked trying to wrap my head around what had just happened.

Six months later, I was a hot mess. It was autumn, exactly one year after I connected with Michael at that Gangaji gathering. The trees losing their leaves and dying mirrored my exact feelings. I was devastated and heartbroken.

Why does my heart contract every time I think of Michael?

One day when I was chatting away with my girlfriend, I realized that I hadn't just loved Michael. I had been in love with him and still was. That is, this was my first time being "in love." Period. I knew firsthand the true meaning of heartbreak because, physically, my heart was in excruciating pain. I felt like an earthquake had shaken inside of me and my heart had tumbled inside-out. I repeatedly blamed myself for not taking direct action sooner in the relationship, knowing all the major red flags waving inside of me.

The first red flag was clearly Michael saying he loved me and then stealing those words right back. I should have stood my ground and cut off the relationship right then. But I didn't, and I was attached to Michael because I was terrified of losing him.

Adding more insult to my injury, Michael decided to stay within this tipsy relationship even after he detached himself from me. Bottom line, I felt like I was his "safety net" person just in case he decided to "settle" when I returned home from India.

I thought, *Why didn't I stand in my power and claim we were over while I had the chance?*

Once again I was in familiar territory, judging and labeling myself as a fool for trying to grab on to a receding relationship.

The remainder of 2009 through 2010, I suffered from unimaginable heartache. I gained at least twenty pounds during those two years, consuming chocolate all day long while wallowing in my own self-pity. I was pathetic. Eventually I was at odds with myself, and I realized I needed to move on. *But how?*

I tried to meditate, however, while attempting to be present by concentrating on my breath, inhaling and exhaling, I inadvertently chanted Michael's name like a mantra, making this an emotionally habitual behavior that carried on for at least a year.

I reminded myself that everything is temporary and these daunting feelings would somehow pass whenever I was ready to authentically let go of Michael, from my heart. Intuitively, I knew I had to brave the fire: not run around it, not dig underneath it, but walk through that burning pain of heartbreak.

Of course this was not easy in any way, shape, or form. However, having faith in myself and my commitment to living in the "now" finally inspired me to heal and move forward with my life.

And even though my emotions were splashed all over the place, I found the will and determination to persevere, no matter how rocky the road to recovery was, to heal from Michael. I knew nobody could save me and mend those shattered bits and pieces of my heart except myself.

As a result, it took me almost two years to recover from Michael. However, there was a huge setback for me in the fall of 2010. Through social media, I discovered Michael had proposed to Jill and they were set to be married in 2011. Just when I thought I was skipping through the healing process, I crashed down hard. Michael's engagement sparked up dark feelings of despair, and I was on the verge of an emotional breakdown.

At the beginning of 2011, I felt a flicker of light peeping through me, circling around my heart, and slowly I started opening up again.

I finally realized I needed to forgive myself in totality in order to forgive Michael in totality. And that simply took time and strong will. I started songwriting to feel through the heartache and pain. The chorus of a song I wrote about Michael: "Ahhh, and then I breathe and surrender. Letting you go is the one true answer."

Mind you, I've only written two songs in my life. However, to my pleasant surprise, writing that sappy song was the first baby-step for me to feel, heal, and forgive myself—and Michael. Eventually, I stopped blaming myself for the repetitive dramas, traumas, and stories of what had seemingly occurred.

My healing process was beyond linear; it was abstract and felt like I climbed a spiral staircase (slow and subtle increments of healing.) My ego was at war with my heart, finding excuses to exploit myself with self-sabotage and mixed messages. I was essentially playing the role of the victim, especially after Michael falsely told me he loved me. As a result, I treated myself as if I were my own arch nemesis.

I knew I needed to surrender and let go. Yet, ongoing negative thoughts flooded my mind. I played the "Michael relationship story" over and over again, magically thinking this would eradicate my pain and suffering altogether. Instead, I was pinned inside the manipulative mind-control game that my ego loved to play with my heart. I was in great disbelief, superficially thinking I was definitely over Michael for months, even years, only to find myself falling back down into the rabbit hole of heartache.

In August 2016, I had the urge to instant message Michael via social media. For whatever reason, I wanted to prove how accomplished I had become seven years after the breakup. The purpose of my text was to inform Michael that I was going to be a guest on an online radio show and share my visual impairment story.

Interestingly enough, halfway through the message I texted, "Why am I telling you about my achievements? It's not like you care anyway. I don't have any idea as to who you are anymore, Michael. Goodbye."

Usually when I send any text message, I thoroughly proofread and edit word for word. However, this time I skimmed over my message and I hit send.

This was my "Amla a-ha moment." I was the one who idolized Michael. I was the one who was attached, obsessed, and felt "the need" to be within this topsy-turvy relationship. I was the one who fell in love with the pretty illusion of Michael, not the actions of Michael.

I cast my own ominous cloud over my head for seven-plus years after Michael and I broke up. Nonetheless, I was the blind one in our "relationship." No pun intended. I was the one desperately seeking to be validated by Michael, when in the end it didn't matter if I had Michael's approval at all. What mattered was that I, Amla, approved of myself. That was the grand finale healing recovery moment for me. From that day forward, I never contacted Michael again.

That last text sent to Michael symbolized the period at the end of this long, run-on sentence (relationship). I forgave myself and

Michael simultaneously in that one bedazzling moment of freedom and unleashing of the heart.

And no, as I expected, Michael never responded to my final text message. However, because I authentically forgave him from my whole heart, I didn't care either way. That message was for me to seal the deal—and heal. And thanks to this significant first love experience, I have learned some amazing, valuable lessons.

Forgiveness is a proactive practice and there is never an expiration date. Just like falling in love with Michael sprung up in a flash, so did my path to forgiving myself and him. I forgave him in an instant—but only when my heart and soul were completely ready to do so.

It may sound cliche, but this was just "a story." The act of falling in love for the first time did not define me; it was merely a part of me. I lived through my fears directly by walking on this nonlinear road to forgiveness moment by moment, day by day, year by year.

I admit that I was hard-hearted and chipped away during my healing years. However, by forgiving myself first and then Michael, I melted into a warmer, more loving version of my Amla-self again.

As Gangaji said, your heart must break down to break open. I did just that. And because I cracked my heart wide open, I had never felt so much lighter and brighter in my life. In fact, because of this particular experience, I now wholeheartedly know that the deeper the pain and suffering, like falling in love for the first time, the sweeter, richer, and more heart-expansive unconditional love I embody for myself.

The process of forgiveness is managed quite differently for each person, depending on the individual circumstances. Symbolically, I was a ticking time bomb blocking myself from forgiving Michael. Essentially, I created my own wrecking ball disaster by:

- First, dwelling on and torturing myself for not knowing any better any sooner.
- Second, my ego was bruised and I never got the concrete answers I eagerly wanted from Michael. Therefore, I latched on and attached myself to "the story" of the experience.
- Third, because I clutched so firmly to "the Michael story," I built a mammoth wall of rage and resentment around my heart. I was livid with myself because I wouldn't allow myself to let go. As a result, it was only when I was honest and authentic with my feelings that I succumbed and began the Journey of Forgiveness.

One key factor to authentically forgive someone is to have no expectations that the other person involved will or will not apologize for their actions. Remember, forgiveness always revolves around healing yourself first. You cannot control how others could or should behave and/or respond to you. You can only control your own attitude and behaviors.

In the end, forgiveness is never about the other person; it's about healing yourself, so that you can move forward without living in your past full of regret. And just remember, this process takes time.

Forgiveness always revolves around checking in with yourself and creating a healthy assessment of where you authentically stand within the specific circumstances.

I've just described my own heartbreak and the Journey of Forgiveness. Perhaps you've had your own heartbreak. Who goes through life without falling in love or getting your heart bulldozed over?

There are various ways forgiveness plays a huge role throughout your life. You can get cut off in traffic; people can physically steal from you; they can cheat on you; they can take advantage of you; they can mistreat you. With that, you may think you can NEVER ever forgive them, or yourself, for allowing them into your life. However, pain is a natural part of life. In the end, you have the free will and choice to snap out of it and move on in order to live your life authentically. Even if/when you get knocked down repetitively, with free will and desire *you can* get back up again. No matter how long it takes, just try. If you think you can, YOU will. If you think you cannot, YOU won't. Additionally, if it doesn't work once, try again until eventually it WILL. After all, a baby doesn't learn how to walk until he or she falls over and over again.

Trust me, if you don't forgive from the heart, you're the one who suffers the most. Always remember, it's perfectly okay to forgive from the heart, yet never forget from your head (the mind), because there is always a lesson to be learned within the act of forgiveness. More importantly, when you forgive someone, it doesn't necessarily mean you invite this person back into your life again. The act of forgiveness is:

A. Doing it from heart "job."
B. Finding acceptance of what occurred in totality without any attachment or resentment.
C. Letting it go and allowing the universe to sweep it all away in due time. The key factor is that you must be ready to FULLY let go. Good luck!

Forgive in order to live, moving onward in sleek strides. If I can forgive Michael with all of my heart and soul over seven years later, there are no excuses as to why you cannot forgive no matter how long it takes. Life is NOW. Make monumental moments and moves without living in any regret.

3 Exercises to Practice on the Journey of Forgiveness

1. One healing affirmation that substantially helped me was the Hawaiian Ho'oponopono prayer:
I love you
I forgive you
I'm grateful
I'm sorry

I added two more of my own mantras to this prayer:

I accept you
I respect you

I repeat these words for myself first, and the second time I send this Hawaiian prayer out to the world. It had such an incredible impact on my own healing process because it seamlessly generated a "let go and let God" attitude. Create your own positive affirmations for yourself and see what happens. The sky's the limit.

2. Writing and journaling. I cannot stress enough how empowering it is to write down your real, raw, and authentic feelings for your personal and professional growth. It's such a healthy outlet to genuinely release, heal, and forgive yourself and the specific experience or person. Try it, it works wonders.

3. One mesmerizing mantra to repeat: "I Let Go, I Let God." Repeat this affirmation as many times as you wish. This has helped me tremendously. Maybe it will help you?

Where's the Light?

I was spending yet another mundane Friday night nestled on my bedroom floor, sitting in front of a mirror in my turquoise snowflake flannel pajamas. I systematically scanned my reflection, back and forth, from left to right.

I had nothing else to do but begin an enlightening conversation with my sparky old-self.

Who is this thirty-six-year-old Indian lady staring back at me? I wondered, as I laid eyes on my pudgy pale cheeks and saggy eyelids drooping over my caramel-colored eyes. Deeply defined crevices created a fork-like design across my forehead. My natural coal-colored hair appeared straw-like, snarled and uncombed, hanging off the curves of my face. My hairline was blanketed in grey highlights.

I gazed at my outer shell and saw an unrecognizable stranger, a woman I'd never seen before. I objectified myself like sticky sludgy molasses over Texas toast, with its tough thick crust on the outside and a spongy, tender center soaked in the rich flavors of melancholy.

I was seriously falling apart, piece by piece, living an existence of polarity because of the tumultuous highs and lows of my life. Once again, the feeling of never being good enough and always receiving the short end of the stick haunted me. I was shackled to hopelessness with no pinpoint of light in sight.

The moment I salvaged enough inner-strength and courage to fix my shredded-up self bit by bit, another part of me became entangled in the dramas, traumas, and misery that has played an active role within the saga of my life.

I faltered to feel, because embracing any emotions felt like someone was charging at me with a dagger, using my heart as their target! I succumbed to a silted and autopilot lifestyle, wearing countless masks and multiple layers of grief and despair.

How did I dig such a deep, gaping hole for myself?

I was suddenly compelled to distract myself. And so I clicked on the television, recklessly surfing through the channels, trying to find a decent program worth one second of my time. I stumbled upon the epic 1997 film *Titanic*, starring Kate Winslet and Leonardo DiCaprio.

This would be my sixth time watching the film. However, this time, I merely caught the last thirty minutes of the movie when the doomed ship plunged down into the bone-chilling waters of the Atlantic Ocean.

The sunken ship's passengers frantically clung to any leftover debris floating on the surface. In the midst of the chaos and commotion, the frightening sounds of children and adults, young and old, fighting for their lives. At this point, Jack and Rose were on the verge of plummeting into the frigid temperatures of the watery abyss.

Reassuring Rose, Jack commanded her to grab his hand, which she did, like a newborn clasping a mother's finger for security and comfort. Due to the hurricane-force rush of murky water, sucking downward with the ship, Jack lost Rose's hand. Jack swiftly swam up to the foamy surface, gasping for air. With sheer panic unfolding in Jack's eyes, he desperately called out for his love, "Rose, Rose!"

Watching this, I clenched my jaw, almost biting off a huge piece of my bottom lip. I gripped my fists tightly as if I were ready for a physical fight. My throat tightened. I gulped hard.

What's happening? I know the ending of Titanic. *Why am I so sucked into this movie as if I were dying myself?*

Once again, I glanced at the television screen. Jack embraced Rose with a full-blown passionate kiss. As I watched this unveil, my heart raced with a pure adrenaline rush, hijacking my body. I was all hot and sweating profusely. And because of my teeter-tottering emotions, my eyes welled up and I was exhausted, just like after a new mother has given birth.

I collapsed down onto my hands and knees in a prayer position. Almost immediately, I shifted my body, curling into the embryo position as if I were right back in my mother's womb. And just like a baby needing her mama for unconditional love and support, I lay sobbing hysterically. Eventually, I crawled up from my fetal position and again knelt on hands and knees, pleading for mercy. My teeth chattered as if it were eight below zero.

"Dear God, I just want to FEEL again!" I shouted.

Meanwhile, Jack lay lifeless on TV as Rose grabbed onto his frozen, tundra-like hand one last time. She cried out her final goodbye, "I'll never let you go, Jack. I'll never let you go."

Within seconds, she freed him physically into the heart of the ocean. Watching this, my body trembled like a construction worker with a jackhammer trying to break open a slab of pavement. This was a true sign of my physical body imploding and exploding with skyrocketing emotions.

I couldn't stomach watching the rest of the movie. I crashed onto my bed, feeling wiped out from the war of me versus my inner demons, which threatened to wash over my entire existence. The waterfall-like tears flushed away the deep-seated residue of emotional toxins as I drifted away into a heavy slumber that somber night.

The next morning, my eyes popped open and I realized that the universe had apparently heard my desperate pleas from the night before. That is, for the first time in two whole years, I felt everything.

Meaning, I felt the most excruciating pain throughout my entire body from head to toe. It's as if my "Amla-hood" collided into an eighteen-wheeler tanker truck head-on, leaving me feeling abandoned, battered, and bashed in due to the catastrophic wreckage.

I had been treated like a nobody, therefore I felt like a nobody. This life-changing epiphany moment left me no choice but to WAKE UP, or to die with gaping flesh wounds penetrating the core of my being.

On one hand, I was relieved because I felt all of my authentic emotions for the first time in a prolonged amount of time. On the other hand, I was mortified and asked myself, *Now what? How do I move forward with my life, feeling like I have sunk into the deep pit of the ocean like the passengers on the* Titanic?

As I sat up erect in bed, I berated God verbally and vehemently.

"What do you want from me? You watch me struggling through the motions of life." I threw my hands up in the air, shaking my head back and forth in a "no" motion.

"Where were you when I needed you? Why am I being punished and going through such endless turmoil? Every freaking time I try, regroup, and get back up from some major setback, I feel set up by you, God, landing me right back into this dead-end tunnel of darkness. When is enough, enough? I want answers, God. I want answers, NOW!"

What felt like an eternity was only a matter of bite-sized moments as I paused and listened. I then paused and listened some more... Nothing but dead silence floating in the air.

There was no singular incident or experience that ignited this derailing and dire path of my deep depression. However, in order to fully comprehend how I hit rock bottom, I must explain one of the most pivotal and painful experiences that uprooted my life, leaving me physically staggering, mentally bereft, and on emotional overload.

In January 2008, I moped around like a dysfunctional robot that needed to be reprogrammed, rebooted, and recharged.

My Amla vitality level was at 5 percent, at best. My favorite "to do" thing was snoozing, because being lost in my "Amla dreamland" involved no effort or contemplation. My luxurious bed represented my security; out on sabbatical.

I remember sluggishly dragging my feet to our family business, which was at most a five-minute walk from our home. It was the dead of winter in Connecticut with the bare trees sprawling towards the thick milkshake sky. I arrived at the store at 10:00 a.m., though my body felt like it was 3:00 a.m. because I was down in the dumps. Although, in an effort to free myself from this debilitating funk, I listened to some good music. Even when I am in the midst of gloom, music always uplifts my day.

Our best-selling products at the store were cotton printed tapestries, also used as tablecloths, sofa and chair covers, wall hangings, and beach blankets, within the United States. We showcased these multi-colored beautiful works of art, hung widespread throughout the store.

More importantly, I purposefully displayed the best-selling exquisitely designed mandala tapestry on the ceiling, so that customers would impulsively buy one.

After I bopped to some of my favorite tunes, I had the inclination to hang up a navy blue and green abstract peacock design tapestry on the ceiling. Minutes prior, a tiny voice inside my head cried, "No, don't do it." I ignored the warning and grabbed some thumbtacks and a step stool in order to hang the tapestry.

As soon as I reached the third and final step on the mini-ladder, my left foot dangled off in mid-air. Within that split second, I knew I was in jeopardy because I had stretched out my right arm too far for me to reach the ceiling. Almost immediately, I lost my balance and footing simultaneously.

I crashed and clunked down to the floor with all of my weight compressed onto the left side of my body. I was numb from head to toe. My entire left leg felt as though somebody was stabbing and jerking pins and needles in and out of me like piercing a voodoo doll. The volatile pain stemmed from my left toes and shot straight up to my left hip.

My gut instinct told me I had broken my leg. I lay there in complete shock. By that time, I had lost all physical sensation throughout the entire left side of my body.

Within a blink of an eye, this freakish accident ripped right through me. And I had no choice but to act independently because I had opened the store for business on my own.

Somehow, after a few moments, inch by inch I crawled my dead weight body to the back door of the store, which was connected to the neighboring barber shop. Because of this blunt force trauma, my caveman instincts kicked in and I radically pounded on the barber shop door, crying for help as if I were on my last breath. Derrick, the barber, opened the door in great disbelief; the sight of my left foot twisted and disfigured, now turned backwards, must have been something you only see in those medical drama TV shows.

Derrick shrieked in distress. I yelled for somebody to fetch some ice. The owner of the barbershop, Charlie, bolted out the door to a nearby McDonald's franchise to get some. Derrick raced to call the ambulance, which tacked on another thirty minutes of my time waiting for the EMT workers to arrive.

I was trembling as Derrick and I were on standby for the ambulance. And within those thirty minutes, while standing like a statue, Derrick elevated my left leg straight up toward the ceiling, applying slight pressure to secure and hold my foot together.

At last the ambulance arrived and the emergency crew scooped me up and swept me away onto the stretcher for another agonizing, protracted, thirty-minute drive to the Hartford hospital. To make matters worse, I was parched, feeling dehydrated during the seemingly endless ambulance ride to the hospital.

Meanwhile, Derrick contacted my mom via cellphone, and thank GOD, she was already in West Hartford, only fifteen minutes away from meeting me at the Hartford hospital. When I showed up at the emergency room, the emergency technician immediately hauled me into an examination room to take X-rays of my left leg.

I recall praying for her to ease up on the multiple twisted-up foot positions that were required to take accurate snapshots of my foot. That being said, the technician held my foot as though it were an intricate mosaic glass vase that had been picked up, dropped, and shattered on the floor. Needless to say, my foot appeared disassembled.

Shortly after this grueling experience at the mercy of the X-ray technician, she wheeled me out through the extended hallways and into my hospital room. My mom greeted me with a glimpse of panic in her eyes. At this point, it was about two hours after my initial fall and accident. My ankle was the size of a tennis ball due to severe inflammation.

Soon after, Dr. Finch, the on-call orthopedic surgeon, walked into my hospital room. He glanced at my foot for a whole two seconds and officially informed my mom and me I had fractured my left ankle. And because my ankle was the size of an inflated balloon, Dr. Finch had no choice but to delay the surgery.

At 6:00 p.m., Dr. Finch sent me home with an unhinged and unfixed left ankle, wearing a tight constrictive cast that clogged up most of my blood circulation from my toes shooting up to my left knee. And, of course, the added bonus feature of pain, pain, and more pain.

As a result of the undying inflammation, I was in limbo-land until Dr. Finch confirmed that he could make the operation happen. During this time, I was snappishly awakened in the wee hours of the night by a sensation that felt like a surgeon was slowly sliding in a giant needle and tearing through the ligaments and tendons of my left ankle. I was miserable.

During my initial emergency room visit, Dr. Finch had suggested that I schedule a follow-up visit to his office to confirm that the inflammation had dissipated enough for him to execute the ankle surgery.

A few days after the emergency room visit, I was off to Dr. Finch's office. When I arrived, the physical assistant guided me into another exam room where he sawed through and unraveled my ankle cast. I was downright too petrified to look at the condition of my injury. The technician then called in Dr. Finch to confirm the status of my foot. Dr. Finch took a sneak peek and instantly said, "Amla, your ankle is all wrinkled up and deflated. A perfect recipe for undergoing surgery. Let's schedule you for the operation."

With that, my fear was somewhat alleviated because I was on my way to getting my foot fixed and getting back on my feet. (No pun intended.) Dr. Finch then offered to show me the updated version of the X-ray images of my left ankle.

"I don't want to know," I said. "Do what you have to do to repair my ankle, Dr. Finch. I simply want to get better."

In retrospect, if I had known the actual, in-depth physical details of my ankle break prior to the foot surgery, I probably would have emotionally and mentally shut down and refrained from the ankle surgery altogether. Therefore, I refused to view the gruesome condition of my ankle.

Eight days after my infamous fall, I underwent a three-hour surgery. Afterward, Dr. Finch greeted me in the recovery room with a cordial and forced smile on his face. He, too, was another no-nonsense doctor with no bedside manner.

"You did okay during surgery, Amla. It took an hour longer

than expected, but if all goes well, you're on the way to healing and recovery," Dr. Finch said.

"Thank you, Dr. Finch," I faintly replied.

Dr. Finch then suggested that my mom and I schedule another post-operation appointment at his office a few days later. The main purpose of this visit was to reassure me that my ankle was healing properly in a relatively reasonable amount of time.

The day of my follow-up appointment, my mom drove me to Dr. Finch's office, forty-five minutes away from my house. When we arrived Dr. Finch's office, I was directed to undergo another slew of X-rays. This time, since my ankle had already been repaired and reconstructed, I decided to view the X-rays of my restored ankle.

"That's what you did to fix my ankle?" I cried.

"Yes, Amla," Dr. Finch replied. "You have nine pins and a plate drilled inside of your ankle to mend your foot back together."

Dr. Finch obviously had no desire to coddle my feelings. My eyes almost popped out of their sockets while viewing these postoperative X-rays of my ankle. Thank God I chose NOT to preview the ankle break prior to surgery.

At last, I was on the road to recovery, literally, one step at a time. Dr. Finch informed me that the anticipated recovery time would include an initial three weeks of bed rest. Thereafter, physical therapy was my number one option for a long-lasting and healthy recovery.

And because this happened to be my first fracture ever, I asked Dr. Finch, "How long does it take to recover and heal from my ankle break?"

"One full year," he said.

"And by following proper protocol, you really think I will get better and reach the ultimate goal of one hundred percent recovery, Dr. Finch?" I eagerly asked.

"As a surgeon, I did my part to fix your fractured ankle, Amla. Now it's up to you whether or not you want to do the work required to heal. It's going to take great motivation and discipline, but if you want to get better, follow the exact guidelines of your physical therapist," he said.

Three weeks later, on Valentine's day, I had my first visit with my physical therapist. And three weeks after the initial physical therapy session, I graduated to wearing a boot, eventually learning how to walk all over again.

I was determined to proactively follow the numerous physical exercises instructed by my physical therapist, Denise, for my optimum health. Hands down, the key ingredient to heal my ankle was physical movement. And when all was said and done, I passed the physical therapy sessions three months later, in May 2008.

Even though I was on my way towards full healing, I still suffered from excessive physical pain throughout the remainder of the year 2008 and into the first quarter of 2009. I was determined to commit to "walking my foot" a few miles a day as a part of my daily regimen to rehabilitate my ankle back into full restoration.

Because of these figurative stricken by lightning types of experiences, not only did my physical body break down, I figuratively "died."

Physically, I died.

Emotionally, I died.

Mentally, I died.

Spiritually, I died.

Hence, this leads me right back to the beginning of this story when I was suffering from this monstrous deep-rooted depression. With that, it included habitual self-loathing and sinking myself down deeper into full-blown depression by watching the *Titanic* in December 2010.

To reiterate, there wasn't one isolated incident that propelled me to land on my hands and knees begging for mercy from God. It was an accumulation of the ongoing "snowball effects" of vision loss, having my heart stomped on, tied to my physical body, symbolically being thrown into the garbage disposal.

1. Physically I died. Not only was I facing blindness (death of the eyes), my physical ankle break symbolizes the roots of a tree being uprooted (my feet).
2. Emotionally I died due to my first time falling in love with Michael, only to be heartbroken in 2009.
3. Mentally I died from rehashing and dwelling on the backlash of emotional dramas and traumas of my heartbreaking experience with Michael relentlessly swarming through my head. And as a form of protection, I was in plain denial and inadvertently swept all of my raw pain and distress underneath the rug, so-to-speak. Hence, mentally, I conveniently escaped from feeling (my depression).
4. Spiritually I died. Meaning I lost all hope and faith within myself and in the higher power, God.

Paradoxically, I was submerged in the pit of filthy waters like the victims of the *Titanic* on the verge of death. That being said, I had no choice but to seize the moment, opening my eyes "wide awake," or quake and combust.

There is no one-size-fits-all to sell-out solutions to a problem.

Therefore, by going through a nearly three-year depression, it was as if I were Humpty Dumpty; that all the king's horses and all the king's men could never put me, Amla Mehta, back together again.

I needed to befriend my own "Amla pain." Meaning face it or fall, over and over again. I felt like I was left for dead in purgatory. As a result, I proactively chose to move forward from the pain and suffering to self-resurrection.

Although, only through time and space did my "Amla healing journey" begin. More importantly, there was always a tiny aspect of me that felt a glimmer of hope and optimism. For instance, I would get up every morning and say: "Today is going to be a good day," and sincerely believe it.

In the end, there was never a "good day" for almost three years. However, the internal light flickering within me steadily fueled and fed my heart and soul. Furthermore, merely by taking one step forward, I felt courageous enough to persevere through these hardcore trials and tribulations, no matter how long or short the duration of full recovery. I was wholeheartedly devoted and empowered to heal psychologically, emotionally, and spiritually. That said, the key ingredients I needed to land on the other side of the rainbow were hope and faith.

A valuable life lesson that I've learned by enduring the depression is: in order to fully save myself, I needed to utilize my own "Amla life preserver" to survive for my own well-being. When your ship is lost at sea and on the fritz, at the heart of the matter, you are the captain of your own ship. You must move onward and upward the best way you can or else you will drown and die.

As a result, I was already figuratively at the ocean pit floor, so there was nowhere else to swim but UP toward the top.

By no means was the journey of self-resurrection easy to forge straight ahead. The path of healing through pain and suffering, whether that be physical, mental, emotional, and/or spiritual, takes dedication, determination, and mindfulness (even if that means pausing from moment to moment). In spite of encountering these particular hardships one after another, my spirit was on the rise with tenacity and grace. Unquestionably, by tapping into the light within me (faith), this represented the key antidote to replenish and renew my soul consciousness.

Just like the wick of a candle represents the source of light, my pure faith served as the fuse, with the limitless capacity to ignite my inner light, expanding and luminously shining on each and every day. Faith is always accessible, not only for me, but for everyone at any time or any place. You merely have to tap into your heart and exercise that muscle. After all, the more you feed your heart with self-love, the more faith permeates through your entire being.

Life is full of high tides, low tides, and tranquil waters. And not one person on this planet is immune from the stumbles, fumbles, heartbreaks, and disastrous falls of life. Ironically enough, that's the only way we, as human beings, transcend in order to ascend.

Life is full of ups and downs and all arounds. Ultimately, in order to outshine life's challenges, you must nurture your mind, body, and spirit and consistently nourish yourself with hope, faith, and unconditional love. The light in me, honors the light in you. Namaste.

3 Exercises to Preserve Hope and Faith in Yourself

1. Positive affirmation, spoken daily.

"I am the Light. Let this light shine through me, above me, and within me down to the core of Mother Earth. I am (your name), I am Light. I am Love. And so it is. And so it is. And so it is."

Practice this affirmation daily, or whenever you feel it's right for you. Remember: what you believe, you receive. The more you practice this affirmation, the more light and love resides inside of you.

2. For all intents and purposes, pray.

Whatever you call it, Source, Universe, Higher Power, angels, speak to your higher power. It doesn't matter how you label it because it all originates from the source of unconditional love. Ask for guidance, peace, serenity, whatever you need. The higher power is everywhere and FOR everyone.

After all, the true miracles come into fruition by maintaining faith from within.

3. Write down at least three things you are grateful for every day.

This feeds and nurtures your soul. Try it. Even if you are at the lowest of all lows in your life, there is always, always something to be grateful for.

Cane Training
and a Crazy Lady

I stepped through the archways of healing between 2011 and 2014. During this time frame, I learned to restructure, re-evaluate, and revitalize myself from a starlight point of view.

And in all honesty, the real possibility of losing my vision slinked its way through the nooks and crannies of my mind, maneuvering its way towards the forefront entrance of my everyday conscious existence. Coping with Gyrate Atrophy was a daunting obstacle, relentlessly blocking my view. No pun intended.

As a result, I felt frozen in fear and realized that I was losing precious time enjoying my ability to see, month by month and year by year. With that, I started to take proactive, and healthy living measures by journaling, walking three to five miles a day, and being conscientious and aware of how I exuded myself as part of humanity.

I was compelled to dive in and prepare for the likelihood of complete vision loss. Therefore, I was ready and willing to leap into action and learn mobility skills by using a cane to be more independent and self-sufficient as a legally blind lady.

In October 2012, I applied for cane training services through the Bureau of Education and Services for the Blind (BESB), offered by the state of Connecticut.

I was assigned to a mobility instructor named Paul. When I spoke with him over the phone to schedule our first appointment in person, we both agreed to meet at my family's business in Connecticut.

I remember being super excited merely by the idea of learning new and innovative skills to enhance my way of living independently by using a cane. I also acknowledged that mobility training would require diligence and great commitment. Furthermore, I was proactively moving forward by accepting that blindness was a real possibility within my future, and I needed to prepare the best possible way by taking mobility training.

The first day of cane training arrived in what felt like only one full breath of time. Paul entered our store with a polite smile.

"Hi, Paul. My name is Amla. It's nice to meet you," I said.

"Hi, Amla. Thank you, it's nice to meet you too. I'd like to start by asking you a series of questions and then I will test and gauge the status of how you currently see," he said.

"Yes, that sounds good. Let's begin," I replied.

Paul started the visual assessment process by asking me to identify certain colors in the store. For instance, he asked me to identify red versus purple. Soon after, he narrowed down the specific color contrasts from navy blue versus black, testing if I had any color vision issues.

Next, we went outside and Paul asked me to count the number of cars I could see and identify from a distance in the parking lot. Lastly, he tested my peripheral vision by asking me to gaze at his nose while he wiggled his fingers closer and closer towards the tip of his nose, coming from all angles like the hands on a clock: 1 o'clock position, 2 o'clock, and so forth. He then asked me to tell him exactly when I saw his fingers in order for him to gage and obtain a general idea of my peripheral visual acuity field, testing both eyes, one at a time.

After we completed the visual assessment segment, Paul said, "Amla, your color and distance vision seem pretty good. Even though Gyrate Atrophy is the number one cause of peripheral vision loss, I didn't expect your vision to be this poor."

I thought to myself, *What? Gosh, darn it. I am losing my vision. Why are you pouring more alcohol on my open wound? Who says something offensive like that to a person losing their vision? Especially my own cane trainer?*

I was furious and flabbergasted. We wrapped up my first session, and as soon as Paul exited the store, once again, I let my tears flow through my sorrow. This one session alone with Paul symbolized a significant "reality check in time" to survey how I would trot through taking life-changing steps to be an independent, efficiently skilled, mobile blind lady.

I immediately questioned the purpose of cane training. *Why do I always end up associating with these authority figures who directly work with the visually impaired and have NO care or sense of compassion for me coping with Gyrate Atrophy?*

And because of that first eye-opening experience with Paul, I would tentatively set up appointments for cane training sessions. However, at the eleventh hour, I would cancel my session with him. When push came to shove, I was downright discouraged and rightfully so, because my first session with Paul blindsided me. No pun intended. To an extent, yes, my vision was poor, but I wasn't ready to hear the truth, or rather, accept the actual outcome of my debilitating eye disease—being sightless. There is a "knowingness" from the heart, and a "knowingness" from the head. I was clearly "knowing about blindness" from my head. Nevertheless, I was living in a dark shade of denial and ego.

It was only one month later when I finally faced the music and experienced my first hands-on appointment with Paul. Nonetheless, from that day forward, I was motivated to devote an hour of my time every week and cane train with Paul.

I must admit, there were times when cane training was crippling, especially during the first few lessons with Paul. My energy level faded fast due to the fact that I mechanically had to exercise and balance between the right and left hemispheres of my brain while being mobile and utilizing the cane.

On the one hand, I told myself to trust and allow my gut instincts to follow through with the specific guidelines of cane training. After all, the cane represents my guiding eyes as a sightless person. On the other hand, I needed to maintain practicality while moving from one place to another, especially by simulating a totally blind lady.

For instance, while climbing stairs and wearing dark glasses that restricted all of my vision, Paul instructed me to count the number of steps on the way up so that I would easily be able to recall the total number of steps on the way down a flight of stairs. The main purpose of this exercise was to enhance my memory skills so that I would develop more self-confidence with an "I can do it" attitude, with or without vision.

Paul also taught me to "hear" the space between the sounds of silence within my environment in order to turn and shift while being mobile and using a cane. For example, if I was moving through hallways, the first step Paul taught me was to use the wall as my crutch. Essentially, tracing it with my cane as I walked from one room to the other. This included months upon months of practice every week with Paul.

Eventually, I graduated to sensing and recognizing the "sound of the empty space," especially while attempting to physically move to another room.

Another example: if I were to walk through the halls of a school, after making a turn from one hallway to the next, in my mind there is absolute certainty that there's an adjacent wall while making the turn (aka a corner). And while my cane represents my eyes, I proactively learned and practiced when and how to turn without bumping into the wall.

This task alone took time, patience, and determination as I learned efficient and effective skills along with energetically sensing and feeling an impending wall as I walked.

Similar to learning how to ride a bike, learning how to be mobile as a legally blind lady develops through consistent practice. Thus, it took me six months to scratch the surface of cane training. Furthermore, these were the beginning stages of "tuning in" and sensing the energetic vibrations of my natural surroundings. And no matter how many times I practiced, I still was on edge and never felt competent enough for this unpredictable journey of cane training. This was especially prevalent while navigating through the spaces and places of an unfamiliar territory, entrenched in complete darkness. That being said, me being Amla, I was my own worst inner-critic, and Paul didn't make me feel any more empowered to learn mobility skills either.

For example, when I showed up for each cane training session, according to Paul, I was a "slow learner" due to the fact that I technically preserved above-average central vision as a legally blind lady. And because I was so nerve-wracked to learn new mobility skills from day one, I set myself up for failure almost every cane training session because of Paul's derogatory comments. Yes, Paul was such a wonderful motivator and mentor for me. No, not quite so.

Ironically enough, because Paul interactively worked with the visually impaired, he admitted that it was somewhat easier for the completely blind potential trainees to adjust to being mobile within the dark, because they had already grown accustomed to coping with little or no vision, with or without using a cane.

Needless to say, almost every time I scheduled a lesson with Paul, I sunk deeper and deeper into fear mode. Ironically enough, the harder I tried in learning how to use the cane, the more I miserably failed at mastering my cane training skills. Hence, while it was already laboring enough being legally blind and experiencing its ripple effect repercussions, I was forced to trek an uphill battle of monotonous and meticulous cane training.

About six months into cane training, I named my cane "Sophia." After all, she's my best friend for life and my loyal companion. When I stroll along the sidewalk with Sophia, I feel empowered, independent, and whole.

Ironically enough, I named her Sophia because I think it's a classy name and I'm a classy gal. "So" means "to know" and "phia" means "philosophy." Therefore, Sophia means knowledge. She represents my guiding light and great strength. After all, SHE symbolizes my personal GPS. Sophia represents my individual freedom to—literally—walk through life with poise and self-empowerment. When I walk with her, we instantly connect and unite as a team.

Sophia uses a marshmallow tip, which rolls and sways back and forth while we walk together. Approximately a quarter of my cane is red and reflects within the dark, so that other pedestrians and vehicle operators can detect exactly where I am located while being outdoors. The remaining portion of my cane is white, so that others instantly know that l am visually impaired. And no, Sophia cannot tolerate when people call her "a stick." The proper name to use to identify her is "Sophia Cane." Or you can call her "Miss Cane" if you prefer to be more formal.

Cane training is extremely complex. It required great awareness and focus to interpret Paul's rigid regimen and methodology of teaching me how to properly walk with Sophia. And, if you didn't guess it already, Paul happened to be one of the stricter cane training teachers.

Throughout this period of cane training, the more external distracting stimuli, the more disoriented I'd be while Paul gave numerous verbal cues to follow while performing the actual task at hand. Additionally, being in complete darkness hijacked the limited vision I already had preserved, which reinforced and solidified one of my ongoing fears of full-blown blindness within my future.

My emotional state of mind clashed with the logical mindset necessary for cane training, and I constantly struggled. To make matters worse, when Paul would outwardly point out, "Amla, you're doing it wrong," I was humiliated, to say the least. Meanwhile, Paul had perfect vision, wasn't going blind, and I know I'm not God, but there is probably a 2 percent chance he will have an accident and actually "be" blind. Nevertheless, based on Paul's actions alone, he had no desire to empathize with my harrowing journey losing my vision. This infused my fiery personality, and not in a good way, either. To this day, I still question Paul's choice of profession.

It's discomforting to have an instructor dictate how I "should or could" see without vision while that instructor is all smiles with 20/20 vision.

Unlike someone who is totally blind, having partial sight means coping with glare whether it's sunny, cloudy, or a rainy day outside. Despite the fluctuating weather patterns, wearing sunglasses only works intermittently. So if I wear them in dim lighting conditions, I see worse or nothing at all. However, if I don't wear them, there are times I strain my eyes to see anything at all due to the intense lights and extreme brightness within my natural environment.

For all intents and purposes, being legally blind is much more difficult than being born blind. That is, when you are blind from birth, there is stability within your life, and obviously your vision never gets worse. Being legally blind, I am forced to adapt to the deterioration of my vision ever-so-slowly. Thus, coping with Gyrate Atrophy is like aging; you don't notice your first grey hair, but over time you notice you have aged because you have clumps of gray hair. The same theme applies to me coping with gradual vision loss.

Because I am currently legally blind, meaning partially sighted, I can still read, choose my own clothes, and see colors (for the most part) effortlessly. However, when the time comes that I cannot maintain self-care as normally and easily as I can today, who knows how I will react?

A year into cane training, Sophia guided me through the swooshing sounds she made when I swept her left to right in front of me. Her distinct sound reminded me of windshield wipers swiping back and forth.

I have been trained to step forward with my left foot while sweeping Sophia to the right, and vice versa when stepping forward with my right foot, I sweep her to the left.

In the end, using Miss Cane is similar to learning how to drive (before I was forced to surrender my license). And just like driver's educational training, you have an instructor teaching you the basics until, finally, you are the driver of your own vehicle. Similarly, practice is the key component in getting better at cane training.

And as the days and months dragged on, once again, Gyrate Atrophy dictated how I adapted and got comfortable learning something new and scary at the same time. That being said, of course I avoided cane training for years. Before Sophia became part of my life, all I yearned for was to be viewed as "normal." Although when I was considered normal and didn't use Miss Cane, I would bump into chairs at a restaurant while others would gawk at me like I was drunk. Now that I use Miss Cane, I automatically become a vulnerability target within the public eye by portraying that I am legally blind by using Sophia, which can be quite intimidating now and then.

I wield Sophia in a way that allows me to explore a full "visual field" comprised of anything or anyone that might obstruct my mobility path. With that, I am the best version of my Amla-self while walking with Sophia.

A year and a half into cane training in 2014, Paul picked me up from my house and we headed off to West Hartford, Connecticut.

CANE TRAINING AND A CRAZY LADY

We yielded our way into a quiet neighborhood where I progressed to cane training on the sidewalks, walking around neighborhood blocks and crossing the streets, all while simulating a completely blind lady.

As we walked, I mindfully listened to Paul's voice and his explicit instructions. At this point, I was moving sleekly through this particular cane training lesson. It almost felt like I was in a trance, listening to nature's sounds: the birds chirping from a landscape that I could only imagine, filled with heartwarming colorful flowers, while the trees whistled in the wind alongside me.

Suddenly, I heard a car horn blare. I jumped up. In seconds, my heart rate spiked up and my hands trembled uncontrollably, all because of that squealing foghorn noise.

"Am I in the middle of the street?" I asked Paul. "Is that why someone honked their car horn?"

"No, you are on the sidewalk," he said calmly.

I thought to myself, *Hello? What are you doing startling a legally blind pedestrian walking on a safe sidewalk?*

Paul remained silent. I heard the car pull over to the curb and stop. Then I heard the creaky noise of the car door opening and slamming shut, and the sound of keys jingling in someone's hands. This person scurried closer and closer towards Paul and me.

I could sense that this person was one or two feet directly in front of us. "What can she see?" a woman's voice asked in some sort of accent I could not place.

Was it Eastern European?

"Can she see at all? When did this happen to her? How?" she asked.

I was dumbfounded. I sensed Paul stiffen, but he courteously responded, "You can ask her yourself."

She asked me a few questions, but at the drop of a hat she redirected her attention back to Paul. I instinctively knew this because I heard her voice redirect away from me as she spoke to him again.

What? I'm standing right in front of you. Why can't you straight up talk to me about my eye condition? I was all hyped up.

As this woman rambled, she explained that her nephew was going blind. That was my cue; I drifted into my own defensive zone. My ears were scorching hot as I felt my face flush.

Should I speak up or not? I fought with myself about whether or not to jump in, just like the game of Double Dutch jump rope.

Amla, don't get all wound up and emotional, I advised myself. *Nothing positive will come of it.*

Why am I always the person who is forced to understand other people's intentions for their absurd actions? I am only accountable and responsible for my own actions. I mean really, it's already challenging enough to cope with the consequences of blindness, but now I'm forced to cope with other people's ignorance? No way!

I was purposely being ignored, to my face, and I would NOT stand by and accept this preposterous behavior.

So, do you tend to ignore your blind relative too? I thought to myself. *Are you afraid of offending him? Because you're doing a great job right now pretending that I'm nonexistent due to your own insecurities and fears.*

Paul nonchalantly stood there, digesting her words. And for the first time in a year and a half of cane training, I felt completely devalued as a human being.

Apparently this woman is the blind one. Apparently I am the unapproachable one due to my disability. God forbid that this physically capable woman would deign to speak to someone who is losing their eyesight.

As she asked Paul a laundry-list of questions and ignored me, I forced myself to imagine a zipper attached to my mouth so that I wouldn't lash out because of her appalling actions. And despite my gut instinct telling me to confront her verbally, I persuaded myself to shut up while this lady yapped away.

I have never felt so slammed down by a stranger in my entire life, which speaks volumes considering all the hiccups I've endured on the path of gradual vision loss. Psychologist Dr. Kip Williams once said, "The feeling of being ignored is equivalent to actual physical pain." I can certainly attest that this is true.

I also wasn't sure if I was more angry at Paul or this crazy lady. To add more gasoline to the fire, when she finally returned to her car and drove off, Paul began making stupid excuses for her.

"It's probably normal in her culture to talk to the 'authority figure' because she had an accent," he said.

"You did NOT just say that, Paul. Are you kidding me? We are human beings first, not brown, black, yellow, purple, or white. I am going blind, not brainless," I cried.

"Well, don't get all riled up, Amla," he said.

"Hello? Nobody deserves to be mistreated because of a disability, religion, gender, race, or sexual orientation. Oh, bring it ON, lady," I said.

What felt like an eternity lasted only about ten minutes. Nevertheless, at that point I'd had enough drama for the day and merely wanted to go home.

As usual, while driving back to my house, Paul stared straight ahead out into the distance as he listened to his favorite country music on the radio. Meanwhile, I still felt rambunctious and continued to rant about what had just transpired.

More mind-boggling, was that this particular incident represented only a tiny fraction of the ignorance I'd potentially encounter in my future as a blind lady. I have engaged with several blind people since this incident and have blatantly seen "normal people" passively question and discount blind people's competence and capacity to preserve a meaningful life.

Nonetheless, having someone dishonor you for being legally blind is not like experiencing awful service at a restaurant. Bad service symbolizes a temporary situation, a mild affront. Worst case scenario, you can choose to never return to that same restaurant. However, while losing my sight, I don't have any choice but to cope with other people's belittling behavior. Needless to say, I am an easy target to downsize because I am disabled.

I also realized that I could never change Paul's or this crazy lady's perspectives. After all, Paul and this ignorant lady could only exude and project their own personas, not anybody else's, which is out of my control.

The late Wayne Dyer has an insightful example he presents in his spiritual teachings. At one of his live speaking engagements Mr Dyer asked, "What do you get when you squeeze an orange?"

The audience giggled. Seconds later, he pointed his finger at a little girl in the front row.

"Young lady, what do you get when you squeeze an orange?" he asked again.

"That's silly. You get orange juice," she replied.

"Yes, that's right, you get orange juice. Not cherry juice. Not blueberry juice. Not cranberry juice. You ONLY get orange juice," he said.

So, what do you get when you figuratively squeeze Paul? You get Paul juice, not Amla juice. Therefore, I will never completely understand other people's ridiculous actions and intentions. However, it's my choice how I respond to other people's behaviors toward me.

To my surprise, I felt even-tempered on the car ride home because I honored my genuine feelings with Paul. I didn't suppress my emotions like I habitually did while suffering through my dark depression years. This goes to show that I had definitely made great strides on my personal journey of upgrading myself.

As Paul gradually rolled to a stop in my driveway, I grabbed Sophia and exited the car. I gave Paul a little smirk, subtly projecting that it was completely acceptable for Paul to be Paul.

More importantly, I learned that I, Amla, could be all of me, blindness or no blindness, despite any outside influential circumstances. As long as I'm not hurting myself or anyone else, I have every right to allow the whipping vortex to whoosh through my "Amla storm" because, sooner or later, this too, shall pass.

While I witnessed Paul reverse out of the driveway, I walked through my front door, literally AND figuratively shutting the door on this blink of an eye, life-altering experience.

Little did I know that this specific incident would haunt me for weeks before I discovered some enlightening insights.

In hindsight, this lady was only spewing whatever programming and/or beliefs and prejudices she had conditionally learned in her life. I just happened to play a critical role in her own story of who she thought I should or could be as a visually impaired person.

Bottom line, even though I was distressed and negatively impacted by this recent experience, I honored my authentic self within the chaos of my emotions jerking me around like a game of tether ball.

Cane training once a week, four times a month, taught me how to be more patient and compassionate toward myself and others. More importantly, by experiencing this crazy lady incident, I have learned to value who I am, despite other people's misconceptions regarding my physical handicap. Needless to say, that's their story, not mine. And the sooner I believe and accept myself for who I am, in totality, the less fired up and offended I will become with other people. After all, I am only accountable for myself, Amla Mehta.

Ignorance can occur at any time and any place. And even though I am on the receiving end of this form of the stigma tethered to visual impairment, the best remedy in response to facing ignorance is the practice of loving yourself unconditionally in spite of other people's actions and behavior.

Just to reiterate, the process of fully healing from negative experiences is feeling your true emotions. After all, physiologically, it's a scientific fact that the human being feels the frequency or vibration first PRIOR to conceptualizing or analyzing what's occurring within the body. A simple example: if you cut your finger, you feel the pain first in milliseconds before you think and say, "I hurt myself."

On the contrary, I am not saying to drown yourself in your emotions. What I am emphasizing is that emotions are powerful in relation to what you feed them. It's like that Native American proverb pertaining to two wolves: "We all have two wolves inside us, love and fear. Whichever one we feed survives."

I choose to survive by nourishing and feeding my Amla self with pure unconditional love. Again, you cannot change anybody else, except yourself. More importantly, you CAN ONLY change:

- Your attitude
- Your emotions
- Your choices
- Your responses

After all, you are the master and producer of your own life. Therefore, any experience, negative or positive, allows the soul's existence to emerge, expand, and evolve, regardless of the outcome or circumstances.

In retrospect, this incident will be ingrained in my consciousness for years to come, because it has taught me to focus my attention on who I am as Amla Mehta, period. Therefore, I have nothing to prove to anyone, not even myself, because I am enough.

By gradually losing my vision, I resonate and "see" souls, not people. After all, the spirit never dies, yet people do. As Forrest Gump says, "Life is like a box of chocolates; you never know what you're gonna get."

That's right, life is full of surprises, negative and positive, and you don't know the outcome unless you try. Be aware and ready at all times for unexpected experiences. More importantly, be like the driver operating your car; move on with a full frontal view of your life. You've got the power. And just like any other steady driver, proceed in life with caution, grace, and ease. Only then can you perhaps set the gauge on "cruise control" because you simply know how to drive your own vehicle on the path of your one-of-a-kind life.

When others tend to project their rudeness or unkind gestures onto you, honor yourself and your needs first, because you matter and nobody knows you better than YOURSELF. After all, nobody can satisfy your hunger except you.

Ignorance comes in many shapes, colors, and sizes, and some people experience it more than others. Such is life. In the end, it doesn't matter who encounters less or more ignorance. What matters is the more connected and balanced you feel internally, the more you can radiate it out to the world. Hence, by embodying unconditional love, you feel more whole and complete, inside and out.

Love IS the answer. Be brave... Be strong... Be powerful... Be ALL of you with love, love, and more love. That's what makes the world so interconnected, unified, and ONE.

No matter what the circumstances may be, always stand tall and be your all, because you deserve the best and nothing less. Namaste.

3 Exercises to Practice While Facing Negativity and Judgment

1. Write a list of at least three qualities you love about yourself every day for at least twenty-one days.
Why twenty-one days? It takes twenty-one days to break into a new habitual pattern. You can also imagine the color pink surrounding you while you write your list. This color represents unconditional love. It will empower you to let your words flow through you and out to the world.

2. Practice this positive affirmation.
"I AM love." Again, what you believe, you receive. Your body will "hear and sense" these simple yet powerful words you tell yourself.

3. Pay it forward by doing at least three kind and compassionate gestures a day.
For instance:

a. Help your neighbor with their groceries.
b. Open a door for somebody behind you at the bank.
c. Write a letter to your loved one sharing why and how they mean so much to you.

Listen to your heart. Good luck!

Barging Through My Boundaries

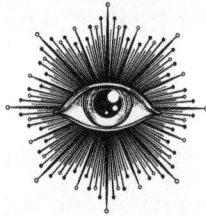

Ever since I was a young girl, I've always had the longing to surround myself with my mom's presence. At kids' birthday parties and social gatherings, the other children would play games outside like kickball, tag, and cops and robbers. However, I chose to play alone, whether it was talking to my imaginary friends or playing girl-power superhero roles like Wonder Woman.

I naturally pretended and emulated her magical and infinite superpowers, deflecting everybody else's negativity by wearing the iconic golden superpower cuffs. Nevertheless, I was in total bliss within my Amla world of wonder, imagination, and creativity. And nobody was allowed to poke or tamper with my dynamic personality.

Playing Wonder Woman also served as my form of protection because I unknowingly was an empath. That is, I couldn't exactly distinguish or compartmentalize my own frequency from other people's energy, although I sure felt everyone else's emotions and feelings.

As a kid, there were several times when I would easily get flustered while playing "house" by myself, and my sister, Parul, would casually walk into the room we shared and ask, "What are you doing?"

Almost immediately my heart rate pumped up because I was so consumed within my Amla bubble; so I felt like Parul accidentally invaded my energy field. As a result, I yearned for my own personal space more excessively than the majority of other kids.

And because I epitomized a true loner, my real-life (and most influential) superhero was my mom. Parul and I were extremely fortunate to have such a nurturing and caring parent within our lives. However, as a kid, little did I know that, like so many other moms, she wore several different hats during the day: as a caretaker, volunteer for non-profit organizations, shop owner, and wife.

Yet, regardless of my mother's other obligations, she always considered Parul and me her number one priority and cared for us girls with such tender and heart-melting love.

While growing up as a kid, my mom's most influential teaching tool she implemented was to share. Parul and I shared toys, our room, and even a twin-size bed. However, I must say, Parul was much more adaptable with sharing than I was. Maybe it was because she was the oldest and felt obligated to lead by example. As the youngest, I strutted my own "Amla walk," embellished with my sassy personality.

Another important code of ethics Mom strongly emphasized was to give unconditionally and to love straight from the heart. Due to our mom's positive influence, Parul and I instinctively knew that when one gives, the heart naturally expands and creates an abundant flow of love for you first, which then automatically stimulates and transcends out to the universe, creating an energetic handshake with the cosmos.

Life revolves around balance and equilibrium. That being said, although giving from the heart is a beautiful act of kindness, if you over-extend and excessively play the role of the "giver," then you might fizzle and burn out too quickly, leaving you feeling drained and exhausted.

On the other hand, always projecting the role of a "taker" and being self-consumed, with an attitude of "What's in it for me?" can be selfish. Ultimately, setting healthy boundaries is one of the key ingredients needed to cultivate a fulfilling and healthy relationship for yourself. Hands down, too much giving or taking is downright unhealthy. That being said, you give because you want to, not because you should or because it's the "right" thing to do. Vice versa: be accepting and grateful when you receive, regardless of whether it's tangible or intangible. After all, it's the thought that stems out of unconditional love that counts.

Since I was taught to be more of the giver, with no expectations in return, I found it taxing to accept and receive at the expense of my own abundance and self-care. With that, throughout my late twenties and thirties, I had a tough time saying "No" with conviction.

I tended to be a "people pleaser" as my preferred way of being nice. As a result, I compromised my Amla-self because I was satisfying other people's needs versus my own. Today, I have realized that setting healthy boundaries for my highest good was, and still is, a continuous struggle in my life.

In 2013, about a year after I started cane training, Paul, my trainer, and I were off to the local grocery store in my town. As usual, the standard procedure for cane training was to wear dark glasses that restricted my entire field of vision. And of course, I couldn't conduct any cane training session without my favorite gal-pal, Sophia (Miss Cane).

This particular cane training session, Paul instructed me to search and find three random items spread throughout the grocery store floor. Paul purposely asked me to find products that I would usually buy at a normal trip to the grocery store: coffee of my choice, iced tea, red plum tomatoes.

Sounds easy enough, right? Wrong.

Even though I still preserve partial vision, I am not oblivious to the fact that someday, when my vision substantially decreases, I won't be able to read any labels, aisle numbers, or find a specific item at the grocery store without any assistance, whether that includes utilizing a scanning device to name a product via audio or asking the clerk to help me find certain items.

And thanks to these cane training sessions every week for a year now, I yearn to be as independent as I can, and I am no longer intimidated to ask for help if and when I need it. More importantly, I have acquired faith in other peoples' intentions and believe they will follow through with their actions if and when I need help. In a nutshell, actively partaking in cane-training sessions prompted me to take more self-care as a visually impaired lady.

So, in order to find the coffee, I walked with Sophia and my grocery cart to the courtesy desk and asked, "Which aisle is the coffee located in?"

"Yes, aisle seven," the clerk answered with a pleasant smile.

"Thank you so much," I replied.

I spun around with my cart and walked toward the left-hand side of the grocery store, toward aisle 7.

At this stage of cane training, I had already mapped out the entire physical layout of the store within my mind, while being fully engulfed in pure darkness. Yes, this is another added time-consuming task to master, which takes practice, practice, and more practice to be more independent and mobile in unfamiliar places.

However, at this point of learning new mobility techniques with Paul, I had polished up my cane training skills in insurmountable ways. Needless to say, I was ecstatic about this amazing accomplishment. More importantly, not only did I master the specific tasks dictated by Paul in the past year, I was fearless, confident, and proud to be the best version of myself as a legally blind lady.

As I was walking toward aisle 7 with Sophia, smoothly sweeping her left to right, I suddenly heard a man's voice and shoes shuffling toward me from behind.

"Ma'am, let me help you," he eagerly said.

"No thank you, I can manage on my own," I replied.

At the snap of two fingers, he stepped to my left, tugged my arm, and pulled me along with him in what felt like a jog.

I immediately panicked and cried out, "Sir, please leave me alone. I am cane training and I really don't need your help." I arm wrestled him, literally.

Within seconds, this incident blindsided me. *Who does this guy think he is, obliterating into my personal space?*

First of all, I am a woman, and as a woman I must be aware and protect myself to preserve my own safety and security. Therefore, when a stranger physically yanks my arm with no hesitation, this is 100 percent unacceptable. Adding more anguish to this particular experience, I was cane training in pitch black darkness. Of course, my senses were heightened and I was naturally sensitive to the slightest sound, noise, or touch. I couldn't fathom what was unfolding right before my "visionless" eyes. I tried to remain calm, however, my emotions clobbered me, preventing me from retaining any form of mindfulness. I was offended, and rightfully so.

"Sir, PLEASE let me go," I cried.

He finally let go of my arm and said, "I work here at the grocery store. I was only trying to help you."

"Thank you, but if I needed help, I would've asked for it," I replied.

For the love of God, he finally walked away and left me alone. Honestly, I didn't care if he was an employee or not. Hello, I am simulating a blind person; I have no ability to scope out who you are. Point blank, it freaks me out when "some guy" tramples on my personal space thinking it's acceptable behavior. Meanwhile, I was furious with Paul because he did nothing to intercede or defend me. A simple "Please leave this woman alone" would have done wonders.

I ripped off my dark glasses and exclaimed, "You should have protected me for my safety, Paul. This man could have easily assaulted me. And yet, you just stood there, lurking around the corner."

"Hello, Earth to Paul? Are you there?" I whispered to myself.

"You figure it out, Amla. This could actually happen in real life," was his insensitive response.

I was stunned. Once again, I was pinned down to deal with Paul's coy behavior. And, to top it all off, my instant reaction was a replay of the crazy lady incident. I didn't know whether I was angrier with Paul or this complete stranger.

While this is a real-life example, there is a distinct difference between how a woman conducts herself, and how a man conducts himself. This barbaric man crossed over my boundaries by assuming I needed help. This guy made assumptions about me, carelessly clutching onto my arm and attempting to whisk me away in an effort to "help me."

Do you know how frightening that is, especially being legally blind? How did this man have the audacity to take my arm without asking my permission?

Personal boundaries exist for a reason, and it's my job to set them forth by speaking my truth. The most outrageous part of this entire fiasco was when I courageously stood up for myself and asserted a firm "No."

This man overbearingly exerted himself to help me whether I wanted it or not. I felt extremely disrespected. Due to the fact that I live with Gyrate Atrophy, and with a vulnerability label of blindness stuck to my back, some people feel they can take control and throw me any which way like a rag doll.

No fail, this man's aggressive behavior terrified me. Here I was, cane training in a grocery store, seeking and embracing my own independence, when this bozo the clown scares the heck out of me because he THINKS he knows what's best for me (based on his actions).

And because of this disheartening incident, I was completely done with our cane training session and asked Paul to take me home. The average person might be inclined to give this particular guy a free-excuse pass. (The excuse pass being that he was only trying to help.) However, this is a classic example of an "Amla boundary buster."

He was just another ignorant person with the intention TO help me but NOT knowing how. First of all, it's important to simply ASK if someone needs help without invading his or her space.

Boundary busters aren't always strangers; it could be anyone you allow (keyword: *allow*) to steal your power, blocking you from being your authentic-self.

By facing ignorance and people careening through my personal boundaries, I have learned that people treat me the way I want to be treated through my actions, not my words.

Here are some wise words of wisdom said by an unknown person:

"Greedy people don't need to set healthy boundaries because they are known as the 'takers.' While 'givers' more or less need to establish dense, thick, underlying boundaries to preserve self-care, self-respect, and self-worth for themselves."

As an adult, I am consistently being triggered and tested to build concrete boundaries with people. Setting healthy boundaries not only feeds my self-respect, it also sets up an opportunity for people to respect me in return. Furthermore, it encourages others to create their own self-care habits, as well as take responsibility for their own actions and feelings. After all, you lead and teach people by being an example.

If you are like me, frequently on the receiving end of a boundary buster, here is some Amla advice.

1. Speak your truth and stand up for yourself. It takes a person with great courage and confidence to speak their truth. You are the master of your life; if you cannot stand up for yourself, who will?

2. Respond to the person trying to bust your boundaries with kindness. Yes, in all honesty, I was rattled beyond belief that day at the grocery store. However, I didn't react radically or irrationally because, as the saying goes, two wrongs don't make a right. Also, as Buddha, the enlightened one, said, "It's not how you react to a person, it's how

you respond." Like Buddha, I responded by speaking my truth, invoking my authentic self.

3. Once you have set up and established your own personal boundaries, be firm with yourself and carry on the attitude that nobody can parade through your boundaries unless you allow them.

Let's imagine that each person represents a state within the United States of America, whether it be Connecticut or California. Every state has different laws to abide by. The same concept applies with people and setting healthy boundaries.

Like the different states, each person has specific standards and a code of ethics to live by and adapt accordingly. Bottom line, what is acceptable for me might not be acceptable for somebody else. The key factor is to exude self-respect first and foremost, while setting healthy boundaries. Only then will others respect your basic staples, needs, and desires.

It takes diligence and practice to discover and uncover what works for you while setting forth healthy boundaries. Furthermore, as you change and evolve, so do your specific standards of boundaries for yourself. The key is to remain vigilant; observe and be mindful of how you project yourself while setting forth healthy boundaries. Like mastering any skill or craft, it takes patience and time to be your authentic and harmonious self while setting healthy boundaries.

Please take note: You might make harsh decisions or mistakes while building boulder-like boundaries, and that's okay. Don't judge yourself. In fact, think of this "downfall" as a detour and zestfully continue on your personal journey of manifesting a healthier and wiser version of yourself.

And because I am continuously evolving, especially by living as a visually impaired person, my boundaries are tested almost every day. Because, according to mainstream society, I am also prone to being a person who always needs "help." And that's exactly why my personal boundaries can "feel" easily discounted and destroyed due to other peoples' behavior, like the grocery worker. Furthermore, because of my visible, outwardly known vulnerability (Gyrate Atrophy), people feel the need to take over by micromanaging every move I make. I find this disheartening because in my case I simply don't see, but that doesn't mean I have no capacity to think for myself independently and make decisions on my own. This is another valid reason why I must implement strong and robust boundaries with people.

In addition, there have been numerous instances when people (usually total strangers) have felt entitled to barrel through my personal space, assuming I am simply "available" at the blink of an eye. Nevertheless, by confronting these people directly, I have learned to stand tall and be the warrior woman I am as Amla Mehta.

More importantly, the more I value myself, the more respect I subliminally demand from other people. Again, you treat yourself the way YOU want to be treated. Thus, by honoring yourself and your own needs, you seamlessly empower and upgrade your own life.

Think of the front door to your home. The home represents your heart and core being. The door symbolizes who enters or exits your home/core being. Of course, the functionality of a door is defined as "to open" and "to close." In a nutshell, you are the one who decides for yourself when and when not to open the door into your heart/home. If you set healthy boundaries by utilizing the lock of the door (meaning using your voice and speaking your truth with kindness), ultimately you choose who enters "your space" and who does not by using your own discernment/"lock and key."

This act alone symbolizes being self-full, not being selfish. Meaning, taking self-care FOR your highest and holiest good. And for all of those beginners setting forth healthy boundaries, just because you "shut the door" on somebody (by exclaiming "no") doesn't mean you're being rude or narcissistic. You are merely taking the necessary precautions to take care of your own needs by setting healthy boundaries for yourself.

Take it from me, setting healthy boundaries can become thorny and complex, especially when you're implementing them through trial and error while using discernment. Handle yourself with love and compassion, because in the end, you're worth the time and effort it takes to set healthy boundaries. Good luck.

3 Exercises to Establish Healthy Boundaries

1. Write a list of your non-negotiable boundaries.
Rely on this list when you feel people are triggering your boundaries.

2. Practice grounding. It's so easy to fall into the trap of your wishy-washy emotions, especially while setting healthy boundaries. Trust me, I am one of those people. However, grounding, meaning doing anything that connects you with Mother Earth, helps you make more effective and wiser decisions. A couple of examples:

a. Walking in the grass barefoot.

b. Chanting the word "*Lam*"; this is the seed sound for the first chakra (energy center within the body) located on the base of the spine. The color associated with the first chakra is red. You could also imagine red streaming into your entire being while connecting, centering, and grounding. Good luck.

3. Learn to say "No" – and to mean it! If you are like me, especially at the beginning stages of setting healthy boundaries, you need to practice saying the word "No." Think of it as parenting yourself for your highest good. If a child darts out into the road, as a parent you might yell and shout, "No, don't do that!" You would do this because you love and care for your child. Same idea with saying "No" for your highest good. You are ultimately taking care of your own needs and desires for your own well-being.

To Speak
or Not to Speak

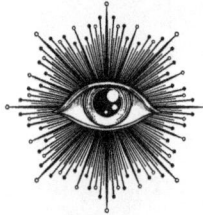

The day had arrived for my annual check-up at the gynecologist's office, I slacked off from getting ready to go on that bright October day in 2018. Despite the fact my body was saturated in fear, I knew if I canceled the appointment altogether I would end up feeling doused in guilt and self-judgment. As a result, I decided to go even though I was experiencing jittery emotions.

Nonetheless, on the drive over to my doctor's office, I felt quite distressed. My driver, a mid-sixties man named Frank, babbled on about politics. My favorite topic? No, not really.

To make matters worse, his car stunk like stale cigarette butts, and because I had never smoked one puff in my life, I felt like I was captured in a moving ashtray with no escape.

Despite being subjected to Frank's relentless ranting, I drifted into my Amla safe haven state of mind on the way to Dr. Fowler's office. I did so by reflecting upon my past and how much I had evolved and grown as a person, both personally and professionally.

I reminisced: *Even though I am following through with this routine doctor check-up, there were plenty of occasions when I would have procrastinated on setting achievable goals for myself, in spite of the fact that I am an independent writer and motivational speaker and I had the option to execute my day any way I wished.*

However, this year in particular, merely by hiring Lori Deboer, my writing coach, I had a crystal clear vision to finish up this first book with a high dose of passion and purpose. That being said, I fully understood how imperative it was to set forth practical deadlines in order to accomplish my day-to-day "To-Do List," welcoming a great sense of achievement.

With that, because I deliberately transported myself into this "Amla A-ha!" epiphany moment, I felt like my old self again. And I was ready and willing to get this exam done, done, and done.

This was my fourth year having an examination by Dr. Fowler, and I valued and trusted her both personally and professionally.

Finally, fruity Frank brought his stinking vehicle to a stop at the office building entrance. We exchanged goodbyes and I was off to take a ride up on the elevator to the fifth floor to Dr. Fowler's office.

I opened the door and, inexplicably, my anxiety level shot up to a high-alert gear because there were people in line ahead of me, waiting. I can be quite impatient, especially when I am stuck waiting in line; it's one of my pet peeves. I would rather do laundry than stand in line.

Oh, well. By this time it was my turn to check in at the front desk. A young woman with dark wavy hair greeted me with a frown. I could sense that she was frazzled, and it was only 9:30 in the morning.

I mechanically told myself, *Amla, be calm. Don't get all caught up in a wild frenzy due to this other person's behavior.*

In addition, I comforted myself by resolving to speak to her with absolute kindness.

This woman curtly asked me to fill out some forms, without any preamble or even saying "good morning." I knew I would need some assistance with this task.

"I am legally blind, and I cannot read the print due to the font size," I said with a composed tone.

She immediately huffed and started shuffling papers around, acting all scatterbrained. At this point, I instinctively knew she had her own preconceptions of me in her mind. She zipped through the intake paperwork, asking me to confirm my address and other questions in a perfunctory manner. Her dismissive behavior made me feel like I was a chore, and a distasteful one at that.

Finally, when she had guided me through to the end of the form, she shoved it toward me and asked me to sign on the line that said, "patient signature."

I stood there for a moment or two scrutinizing the form while she regarded me with disdain. I was not physically capable of seeing the line in question; the whole form looked like one humongous blur.

I took a deep breath.

"Can you please mark an 'X' alongside the empty space to the left of the text, so that I can see where the exact line is located?" I politely asked.

Before I could utter another word, she stole those papers away, acting like a child not receiving his or her favorite toy.

"I'll have the person in charge of registration help you shortly," she snapped.

I stood there, flabbergasted. I told myself, *This lady is obviously annoyed with her job, but what would she do if she were legally blind and needed help?*

Welcome to my world of frustration, which comprises most of my everyday life.

Although I was an emotional basket case at the front desk, I mindfully walked back to the waiting area and plunked myself down in the chair, waiting for the manager to assist me.

Ten minutes later, the woman called out my name, drawing it out in two distinct syllables, "Am La." She made it sound like "Am" was my first name and "La" was my middle name.

Sometimes people confuse my name, thinking it's "La," because they misinterpret "Am" as "I'm" and "La" as my real name, as if I were introducing myself by saying, "Hi, I'm La."

Who would've thought? And just for clarification purposes, my name is pronounced "Uhm-la."

Nevertheless, I was all wound up. However, I swallowed her words down, bit my tongue, and shadowed her into her office.

The manager was maybe in her fifties, with a British accent and shoulder-length brown hair with blonde highlights. I was fighting to keep my emotions in tact, but I felt them floating up to the surface.

Before this woman had any chance to speak, with my sappy voice I pleaded, "I am emotional, and I'm about to cry."

"Oh, it's ooh-kay, it's ooh-kay, don't cry," she said in her British accent, drawing out the "o."

I hardened. "No, it's not okay. It's not okay," I replied sharply. "Did you speak to the lady at the front desk and find out what happened and why I'm being forced to talk to you and mediate this situation?" I asked.

She glared at me like I was the ruthless instigator and clearly at fault.

"Your receptionist is inconsiderate and narcissistic." I continued, "I was mistreated by her. She wasn't professional at all. She had no genuine intention of complying with my request for assistance. And yes, I admit I am taking this personally. However, it's her job to help me as a patient, especially when I directly asked her for it," I said.

She fiddled with her reading glasses acting all aloof.

"All I asked the receptionist to do was mark an 'X' where I had to sign the document, and she was so annoyed she ripped those papers away from me before I even had the opportunity to explain myself," I added.

The woman glued her eyeballs at me for moments that felt like a lifetime. Finally, she said, "Well, maybe the receptionist thought you were asking her to sign the form."

"What? Why would she 'maybe' think that?"

Mind you, I am not an invalid. I knew it was my responsibility to sign the papers, period; there was no misinterpretation on my part. I would not allow this lady to pull the wool over my eyes.

Once again I asked, "Did you even consult with your reception-ist and attain a solid explanation of her side of the story? You keep on saying 'maybe this' and 'maybe that,'" I said.

"No, I have not talked to her," she answered.

What kind of ridiculous statement is that? I thought. Why was she making useless excuses for her staff members?

At this point, my strings were all tight and wound up like a yo-yo. *How dare this woman make excuses for her employee not con-ducting her job tactfully?*

I've had people at Dunkin' treat me with more respect and kindness than these two people who were not placing the patient's care and needs as their first and foremost priority.

"I am not signing anything. I will sign these papers with Dr. Fowler," I said sternly. I had faith in my doctor to resolve this whole mishap softly and smoothly, like cutting rich butter.

"These papers have nothing to do with Dr. Fowler. I want you to have the best possible care, Amla. By not signing these forms, you might be cutting off your allotted time to be examined by Dr. Fowler," she scowled.

Oh, you did not just say that! What's up with this lady if I shave off time with my own doctor? I thought, *Is this my problem or yours?*

I was bolted tightly to the ground and was not about to buckle.

"I will sign the papers after speaking with Dr. Fowler," I repeated once again.

She shrugged and said, "Fine."

But it obviously was not fine. Nevertheless, I refused to sign the documents and I dashed out of that British lady's office, back into the waiting area.

I couldn't fathom the unnecessary drama merely because I had made a reasonable request and asked for help due to my visual impairment. And these so-called office "professionals" were all wired-up because I had inadvertently created massive uproar in their ideal, wrinkle-free day.

God forbid their day was disrupted because of me being an "inconvenience." I felt like a chunk of chocolate on a factory conveyor belt. Meaning, I should be all subservient, orderly, and move it right along without any glitches in the production line.

Finally, an assistant nurse called my name and ushered me into Dr. Fowler's examination room. With her gleaming smile, the nurse guided me through her routine assessment, jotting down my height, weight, and blood pressure measurements.

My instincts told me she knew I was on the verge of tears. Although, compared to those other two employees, this young woman was an angel, a breath of fresh air, treating me with compassion and understanding.

The nurse gently directed me to change into a standard gown. And, despite the fact that I was so provoked by what had just occurred, I had strong faith that by expressing my truth with Dr. Fowler, it would be smooth sailing thereafter. After all, she was my doctor, one in whom I confided and revealed my most private information pertaining to my health.

When the nurse finally exited the exam room, the emotions trickled in as I reclined into the chair, and I felt my face crumple. With sorrow spiraling up to the surface, I covered my eyes and sobbed away. At first I fought it, but soon after I surrendered and let the tears flow right through me.

After a few minutes, I tried to stall and refrain from weeping because I didn't want Dr. Fowler to intrude into my personal space, both emotionally and psychologically. Feeling somewhat relieved, I inhaled fully, let out a big sigh, and exhaled from my belly and out through my mouth.

Boy, did I need that deep release, I thought.

In retrospect, I saved some of my unshed tears and emotions for Dr. Fowler, because I believed she would naturally represent a safe outlet for me to be all of my sloppy, emotional, authentic self.

At last, I heard a faint knock on the door and I said, "Come on in."

She greeted me with her usual cheerleader smile and proceeded to sit on her wheeled stool. Meanwhile, I felt my eyes well up all over again. This was my one-time chance to speak my truth without being all blubbery, yet my emotions overpowered me once again.

I couldn't resist it anymore so I confessed, "I'm about to cry."

"Oh no, Amla, what's wrong? Don't cry," she said.

"I need to cry to release and let go," I said.

Her eyes appeared glazed as if she didn't hear me, and she repeated the question, "Why are you crying?"

I gave her a detailed rundown of what had occurred with the first receptionist and how she refused to help me, despite the fact that I had requested her assistance. I then described how the office manager had redirected me to sign the form, and I decided not to sign anything because I wanted to ask Dr. Fowler to iron out these unforeseen circumstances.

Dr. Fowler skimmed through the papers. "Amla, I don't care about these documents. These are only important for updating the most recent data about each patient," she said.

She smiled, and I sensed she was trying to cajole me into letting this entire incident magically disintegrate and disappear.

"All I yearned for was for the first receptionist to listen to me and follow through with my humble request. But she snatched those papers away so conveniently, I didn't even have the chance to swallow and be heard, as is my right as a patient," I exclaimed.

Dr. Fowler was being defensive and close-minded as she crossed her arms and legs while fixating on me accusingly.

Within that split moment, it dawned on me: There I was, vulnerable and exposed on all levels. And this was "the moment" to speak my whole undyed truth.

"Amla, my staff would never have purposely hurt you, and they wouldn't do anything to make you feel less competent," she said with a frosty tone to her voice.

I couldn't believe what I had just heard. Once again, my emotions cascaded over me.

How can Dr. Fowler, a person whom I trust and in whom I regularly confide my most personal information, NOT consider and consult with her staff to thoroughly investigate what exactly transpired?

"Amla, you shouldn't wear your emotions on your sleeve," she said, trying to hush me.

I couldn't believe how dismissive Dr. Fowler was acting by undermining me as a patient, to speak my truth.

"Well, I do, and I am proud of that," I proclaimed.

What I wished I had said out loud was, "Who are you, Dr. Fowler? You are not the doctor I have interacted with in the past. I have every right to be emotional, especially with you, my own doctor. Why should I be forced to validate my emotions?"

Big deal, Dr. Fowler, your patient is emotional. I'm sure it's not the first time you've encountered a patient like me, and I'm sure it won't be your last, I thought to myself.

She stood up, turned her back to me, and began washing her hands at the sink, nonchalantly escaping from any confrontation.

"You know, this is exactly like the 'Me Too' movement," I said.

She whipped around so fast, her eyes practically bulging out of their sockets.

She shook her head side to side. "No, Amla, this is NOT like the 'Me Too' movement," she exclaimed.

"If you would just listen to me, I will explain how this incident is similar and runs a parallel theme," I replied. "I might not have been physically violated, but the 'Me Too' movement is all about having the right to be heard and validated, using your voice as a platform to raise consciousness into the world. That it's never okay to be physically, emotionally, or mentally abused by anyone," I exclaimed.

She crossed her arms again and gave me a dubious look.

"In addition, one has absolutely every right to raise awareness by speaking up, and this morning I didn't feel heard, respected or validated enough by any of your staff members to inquire about what had actually occurred. Ultimately, I felt disrespected and disregarded as your patient. Dr. Fowler, if I didn't speak up today, how would you know the real truth behind the curtains of your facility?" I asked.

She remained tight lipped, so I continued. "It's not like I have a trail of people behind me advocating for the blind. Who's going to defend and stand up for me, except me, the blind lady? Therefore, I am being my own advocate for myself, the blind, and on a macrocosm level, all of the disabled and handicapped," I exclaimed.

"Everybody has problems, Amla," Dr. Fowler said. "You're not the only one."

I thought to myself, *Did I ever once imply, 'Oh, woe is me, have pity for the legally blind lady?' No. I am outraged because I asked for assistance, and instead I faced full-force ignorance and lack of compassion, splattered all over my face from your staff, and now you, Dr Fowler.*

Would you make this exact same remark to a patient who has cervical cancer? Oh yes, Miss Jane Doe, you have cancer but everybody has problems. How absurd is that? What a supportive and compassionate doctor you are, Dr. Fowler.

Oh, if only had verbalized those thoughts at the time!

"Dr. Fowler, in this entire conversation, have I ever said or implied this is solely about me? No. I am speaking up because I just experienced full-force ignorance, disrespect, and lack of compassion from your staff," I cried.

Apparently, Dr. Fowler didn't care too much for the ideals I was professing based on her verbal and nonverbal actions. What transpired was inexcusable and I was not tolerating any of these shenanigans by zipping my lips. There is a divine time and place to speak up–and a time to shut up. And, without any doubt, I chose to speak up in this moment.

The truth never changes its colors, or wavers up and down; lies do that job. There's a refined yet subtle flow streaming through the current of truth. More importantly, truth symbolizes the essence-like nectar to replenish and nurture the nugget of the soul. Therefore, I was not only speaking up for me, but for those who cannot communicate and literally have no voice.

I am human and I merely need and want to be understood. More so, my heart feels frayed and ruptured when I am not validated as a person because of my disability. Dr. Fowler's next words left me outraged.

"Amla, you also don't look blind."

Huh? I thought to myself. *What are blind people supposed to look like? How are we supposed to act? Should I be wearing a sign all day long stating that I am legally blind? There is no one-size-fits-all role model for the visually impaired. Is every doctor similar to how you perform your practice and area of expertise?*

It's not my job to announce my disability to everyone under the sun, whether I fit the crafted "mold" of a blind person or not.

I only reveal my visual impairment when it's relevant, like it is in this scenario.

In order to defuse my feistiness, Dr. Fowler finally nodded up and down. "At least you expressed yourself."

Shortly afterward, she resumed and finished my pelvic exam. *Thank God it's finally over*, I thought. I couldn't get out of that office fast enough.

In retrospect, I could have stormed out of Dr. Fowler's office immediately after the first receptionist hissed at me and was unsympathetic towards my needs. However, I continued with the visit from beginning to end, including finishing up with the physical examination, because I truly believed that Dr. Fowler would empathize with me as her loyal and committed patient.

Afterward, as I waited for Frank to pick me up, I was disoriented and outraged. *What was that all about?* I thought to myself.

How do I resolve this ongoing saga of facing oppression, ignorance, and insensitivity due to the ripple effects of Gyrate Atrophy?

After I had consciously made the bold decision to stand up for myself, yet I felt like I was considered a "problematic patient" not only with the staff, but also with Dr. Fowler, based on her derogatory behavior.

Interestingly enough, the more I speak my truth with people, the more eyebrows are raised in response to my words, literally. Truth be told, that's their stuff, not mine.

After all, I am not responsible for how other people receive or hear my words. I am only accountable for myself. As long as I am speaking my truth straight from the heart with sincerity, I will always express myself genuinely because the truth always prevails. Maybe not the way one might have imagined, however, speaking my truth allows me to be my Amla authentic self and I wouldn't trade that for the world.

While I might be labeled as a legally blind lady, I see crystal clearly internally with a satellite dish point of view of the world. That being said, one of the most significant gifts of being visually impaired is that it allows me to pierce through the lies, deception, and manipulation from others because I see with my third eye, located smack dab in the middle of my forehead, between my eyebrows. Nonetheless, I "see" perfectly, just not the way most people do.

Unfortunately, this despicable incident haunted me for the next twelve days. Therefore, I decided to call Dr. Fowler's office and terminate my patient care with her altogether.

"Hello?" the receptionist responded to my call.

"Hello, my name is Amla Mehta, and I'm choosing to withdraw from all of Dr. Fowler's services as my gynecologist. I am one hundred percent confident with my final decision," I said.

"Would you like to speak to the head manager?" the receptionist asked.

"No, I am not speaking with that British manager," I said.

"No, no, this would be a man by the name of Mark," she replied.

I paused to consider her offer. "Yes, I'd be willing to speak to him and try to resolve this issue," I said.

"One moment, please," she said.

I thought to myself, *Where was this woman when I needed assistance at Dr. Fowler's appointment?*

The manager answered the phone and, in an even toned-manner, said, "Hello, Mark speaking."

After formally introducing myself, I gave Mark a quick

play-by-play summary of the recent unfortunate experience as if it had only happened minutes prior.

"I initially called the office to end all patient services with Dr. Fowler. However, the phone receptionist convinced me to converse with you about my experience twelve days ago. And Mark, I acknowledge it's twelve days later, but I am still affected and disheartened by the way I was negatively treated as a patient," I said calmly.

"It doesn't matter if it's twelve days or six months later," he said. "This affected you as a patient and that concerns me. I will definitely talk to these three staff members and reinforce the code of conduct and how maintaining empathy with each and every patient is imperative to how our office efficiently and effectively represents itself," he said.

"Thank you," I replied.

"I cannot guarantee they will apologize for their behavior, but they will definitely be confronted by me about your recent negative experience with them. Amla, you have every right to feel angry about this situation. Nobody deserves to be treated like they are invisible," he said.

I heaved a huge sigh relief. I could literally feel Mark's compassion transmitting through the airwaves of the phone. At last, I, Amla Mehta, felt understood and validated.

And because I had experienced these extreme emotional dramas and traumas, I honored my final decision to seek out another doctor. Hands down, I'm proud that I not only raised awareness, but that I did so with integrity and self-respect. In addition, I didn't just walk away consumed with fear; I challenged myself and fought for my own justice because nobody else will do that for me except me, myself, and I.

One should never refrain from expressing their thoughts and

feelings just to keep the peace, especially if it relates to something as powerful as serving your highest good. As long as you communicate your opinions and beliefs with dignity and respect, you have every right to object to those who suppress and/or oppress you in your life.

The key factor is that you maintain heightened awareness while using discernment; it's your choice when to assert yourself and when to walk away and surrender. Communicating your core beliefs, whether it's personal or business, is a wholesome and an effective way to establish solid healthy relationships in your life.

It was quite evident to me that Dr. Fowler didn't *want* to invest the time required to understand me, nor will she ever, in my mind.

People think and behave based on their own conditions and belief systems. Therefore, it doesn't surprise me when those false perceptions spill over onto me. Frankly speaking, from my personal hands-on experience as a disabled lady, I tend to be treated as a bug-bite irritation because mainstream society labels "the disabled" as weak, an easy target, and a so-called "pushover" in virtually any situation.

God gave me a voice and I certainly know when to speak up and when to stay still, calm, and quiet. You may not be disabled like me, but there is always an opportunity for you to express yourself and be heard if you strongly and passionately feel your sense of self has been stripped down to your bones. Trust yourself. Even when you might be shaking in your boots while speaking your truth, trust me: go for it. You deserve to be heard. Period.

I might not have received the ideal outcome of what I was hoping for from this particular incident; however, I wholeheartedly appreciate and value myself for speaking my pure truth.

In the end, it doesn't matter how Dr. Fowler or anyone else

perceives me. If I can genuinely look in the mirror and smile at the sassy, intelligent, and charismatic person staring right back at me, so can you.

Don't define or judge yourself based upon other people's actions and/or perceptions. You define you, based on your attitude and your actions. Take pride in who you are, and that's all that matters.

Good luck!

3 Exercises to Enable You to Speak Your Truth

1. This is my own Amla therapy and it works. You might laugh at me, but…I scream.

Of course, it's in a safe environment. Screaming literally shakes up your throat chakra. And just like any physical exercise, by screaming, you are literally *moving* the stagnant energy within the throat chakra (letting it all OUT). (I usually blare the radio in the car when **I scream**.)

Honestly, it only lasts about five minutes maximum because it burns up a lot of my energy.

A little friendly disclaimer: Only do this in a safe and protected environment. Don't yell/scream at people or your boss. For all intents and purposes, scream when you are alone. Good luck!

2. The 5th chakra (energy center) located in the throat area is connected to speaking your truth. The seed sound of this chakra is "*Ham*" (pronounced "*Hum*"), and the color associated with it is blue.
Repeat this sound as many times as you wish. This is very effective, especially while at work or if you're in a stressful situation where you need to conserve your energy.

You can repeat this in your mind anytime. It doesn't have to be out loud as long as you are feeling the frequency of the sound within your mind, body, and spirit.

3. Communication is key, including self-talk.

My personal "Amla therapy" consists of gazing into the mirror almost in a trance-like state of mind (at least as long as I preserve partial vision) and allowing myself to be unleashed using my words.

I talk to myself about anything and everything that matters to me. And sometimes my words don't even make sense. However, it's a healthy outlet for me to be true to myself.

Bottom line, doing this helps you unwind and unpeel the layers of you. Just like peeling an onion, moving closer and closer to the root and truth of who you are. More importantly, by talking out loud directly in front of a mirror, this helps you literally see and embrace your pure authentic-self. Good luck!

The Gift of Lifts

After officially being declared legally blind back in 1996, I received documentation from the state of Connecticut as a form of proof when I require special services like public transportation.

I won't paint it lightly; being forbidden to drive is a troublesome matter, especially when I lost my driver's license on the heels of turning twenty-two years old. After all, driving represents your freedom to make choices pertaining to when and where you'd like to go on your time, not on anybody else's time.

In the state of Connecticut, being mobile and independent can be problematic for people with disabilities. Unfortunately, the state does not provide sufficient public transportation for those living in the periphery of the Hartford area, like me. One of my consistent struggles is my need to ask for rides for mandatory appointments, doing errands, and even being socially active.

There's a van in our town that travels within a five-mile radius, which enables me to fulfill errands like going to the bank, grocery store, and local shopping. I am required to schedule my ride from 9:00 a.m. to 12:00 p.m., twenty-four hours in advance, allowing me to use the service for my individual needs. The van itself runs from 9:00 a.m. to 4:00 p.m. on weekdays, nothing on evenings, and limited hours on weekends.

In a nutshell, at approximately 3:00 p.m. I need to plan my time accordingly to return back to the van stop, or I turn into a pumpkin. And because I am under a "curfew," I'm frequently eying the clock to reassure myself that I'm able to catch the van ride home. As one would expect, it's no picnic trying to be spontaneous with such an arrangement. I'm required to plan my days well in advance. Yet, I must admit, it's better than having no available public transportation services at all.

In my leisure time, I enjoy going out to listen to local bands or participate in holistic events like yoga, drumming circles, and aromatherapy, although these specific activities usually don't occur during the van's routine schedule. For instance, my yoga class is only two miles down the road, and I must ask for personal rides nonstop. That being said, I am blessed that my yoga buddies, Arlene and Tom, insist on and assist in giving me a ride to and from yoga with no ex- pectations in return. We don't always participate in the same classes; however, my friends are always reliable with rides to the yoga center. And I am grateful for their genuine kindness and compassion. My family cares enough to drive me when they can, but I don't want to tax my aging parents too much.

One would think receiving a ride from someone would be a simple task. But this whole "ride thing," in my eyes, fuels more hard- ships. For better or worse, asking a person for a ride launches you into psychological territory that comprises how the person treats others based on their own actions. Furthermore, it affects how they dole out their time and reveals how they honor their own commitments, aside from helping other people in need, like me.

For example, in 2015, my friend Joy, who practiced yoga with me, once said: "Amla, if you ever need a ride back home from yoga class, I'd be happy to give you one."

I was quite moved by her sincere gesture. "Thank you so much. I appreciate it and I will definitely consider your offer in the future," I kindly replied.

Joy and I saw each other twice a week at our 5:30 p.m. yoga class. Six months into our friendship, I accepted Joy's offer. I intentionally texted Joy early enough for her to reply with a simple "yes" or "no" answer. After all, there are no guarantees that someone will be able to give me a lift. A few minutes later, she replied with a resounding "yes."

I was thankful and replied: "Great, see you at our 5:30 p.m. class."

After a gentle, restorative yoga practice, Joy jerked me by the arm and practically pulled me out the door. She nudged me down the stairs like she had an emergency to resolve. "Come on, come on," she said, as I cautiously navigated my way down the stairs. At this hour it was considerably dark. Therefore, my night blindness kicked in, which made it much worse moving my way down the stairs. I took one step at a time, literally, because I was fearful of experiencing a terrible tumble. Joy continued and lugged me along. However, I kept my mouth shut because I didn't want to cause any unnecessary conflict between us.

We walked to her car in the parking lot, hopped in, and Joy and I were off to my house, a measly two miles down the road. We were chatting away as usual, and out of the blue, she gave me a sidelong glance. And in a slightly snooty tone, she said, "You know, I am going out of my way for you by giving you a ride."

What? Here is a woman who offered me a ride home. And when I ask her for the first time ever, she makes a rude remark like that?

Not only did her comment disturb me, but she also expressed herself as if she were giving me a blood transfusion or something, rather than driving me home two miles.

First of all, she wasn't obligated to say "yes" when I asked her for a ride. She could've easily said, "No, sorry, Amla, I cannot give you a ride today," especially within a simple text. "No" is spelled with two letters. (A five-year-old could've sent the text.) Instead, Joy had said "yes." However, she accepted to give me a ride with a passive-aggressive twist. Needless to say, I felt treated as if I were a pebble on the side of the road. As a result, I instantly reevaluated my friendship with her.

When I feel rejected and hurt, I retreat into silence. Hence, I was mum during the remainder of the car ride home. That said, she couldn't have pulled into my driveway any faster as I expressed my goodbye to her courteously.

To add more agony, she cut me off, waving me out of the car. "I am in a huge hurry home because I need to go to the bathroom," she said.

I thought to myself, *No wonder she whisked me down those steps at the yoga center. Why didn't she communicate that she needed to go at the yoga center, to save herself from any further discomfort?*

If Joy couldn't make a simple decision about whether or not to use the bathroom at the studio, how could I presume she would follow through and graciously give me a ride home? This woman clearly could not make concrete decisions based on her actions. Unfortunately, for whatever reason I will never know, Joy displayed her irritability by using me as a scapegoat.

I barreled out of her vehicle, shaking profusely. She skedaddled out of my driveway as I was searching for my keys, attempting to unlock the front door of my home. I then darted into my bedroom, masking my slippery emotions from my family. I thunked onto my bed and let the tears roll. This was and still is an ongoing "replay button story," regarding receiving rides from people.

I had considered Joy a true friend. However, within seconds she managed to place a dent in our friendship. This incident punctured my heart because I'm not a moocher, nor do I expect favors from people at all times. Sure, it was "just a ride" for some, but for me, as a disabled lady, rides are imperative for my personal and professional life.

The fact that I am handicapped makes my life much harder to establish and solidify sincere and trustworthy relationships. As a result, I regularly feel like I'm being figuratively short-changed with people because of my visual impairment. It's no wonder why I question people's genuine intentions in relation to me needing and receiving rides.

Because of frequent incidents similar to the one with Joy, occasionally I question: are people helping me because they expect something of equal value in return? Sometimes people only help conditionally: to feel superior and have their egos stroked when they are rewarded for their common good deed. In addition, they exude entitlement to feel more able/capable while they passively view me as inferior because of my visual impairment.

As a result of Joy's snub, I had no desire to continue my friendship with her. That being said, the following weeks in yoga class, Joy would attempt to communicate with me but I would reply with short, clipped answers. Eventually, she caught on and we both drifted apart.

Because of disappointing experiences like this, time and time again, I have mixed feelings when people offer me help. On the one hand, I tend to have faith that the person will follow through. On the other hand, the minute someone offers help, such as giving me a ride, I easily get disgruntled and believe I will be "let down" by the driver not executing my need for a ride.

Flux and conflict is inevitable. The key is whether or not one chooses to be a patron to the dramas and traumas of life. In this case, although I was inconvenienced by Joy's behavior, I blocked further pain and suffering by walking away from the friendship altogether. I honor and value my own needs as my number one priority. True friends show me that they care through their actions, not their words.

If you are like me, you may feel the need to honor your authentic self, despite the outcome. Although, I'm only human, and there have been plenty of occasions where I have felt my firecracker, impulsive self bubble up to the surface. Yes, sometimes I struggle to know when and when not to react or respond within the moment.

However, when you take a step back and view the situation from a bird's-eye view, it's a more mindful way to respond and convey your message. And even though venting and purging your words may perhaps ease the initial sting, ultimately, an impulsive and emotional reaction is never helpful in the long run. I prefer to let the initial scenario simmer a good couple of days until I develop a more mindful response. Nevertheless, when I take the time and space to digest the situation, I set myself up for more profound insights, which always serves my highest and holiest good.

Why not express my raw emotions with people while being fresh in the moment? Because, even if the person in question were insincere, unkind, rude, or manipulative, an authentic relationship is a two-way street. If I only respond with the same thoughtlessness and indifference to people's ignorance, there's less opportunity to improve and resolve the situation. In a nutshell, if I act volatile toward them, I'm merely embodying their nonsense and negativity as my own.

Through trials and tribulations, it took me several years to develop the maturation from being emotionally reactive to being mindfully responsive. I have learned to be genuinely honest, using a kind tone, not a kiss-butt tone. There is a huge difference.

Responding mindfully is a proactive way to deflect other people's negativity. And if you can respond with kindness, you are naturally bringing forth accountability and responsibility through your own actions. With that, if I am not responsible for my own actions, how can I expect the other person to do the same? That said, what other people do or say is not my problem. However, what I say or do is definitely my problem.

Although these unexpected negative circumstances happen, I still maintain a positive outlook and hope people are being authentic when they offer to assist me. More or less, I have no need to ponder: *Does so-and-so really want to give me a ride? Do they mean it? Do they not mean it?* It's not my job to supervise someone else's true intentions. There's a common saying: "different strokes for different folks." Just because I had a negative experience with Joy, doesn't mean everybody else who offers me help will project themselves the same exact way.

Furthermore, if someone doesn't follow through with a promise or commitment, I am accountable for authentically communicating how their actions affected me. And I manage to do so with kindness and compassion.

I've become so accustomed to people not following through, or being dismissive, that when they do commit, I am pleasantly surprised. On the flip side, I try not to take it personally when/if the driver doesn't show up, and I have learned to always have back-up plans. At most I have a Plan A and a Plan B, and if Plan B breaks down, I make the final decision to cancel my plans altogether. A tough lesson to learn, but I believe in respecting myself with dignity rather than to ask five people for a ride. It's just not worth it.

Within the experience with Joy, I withheld my exact feelings because this incident exemplified a superficial undertone, and saving it wasn't worth my breath. I surrendered and instantly knew Joy wasn't in my contact treasure chest list of friends anymore. For me, real friendship means that giving and receiving comes easily, straight from the heart. And being authentic means saying "yes" when you mean it and saying "no" when you cannot commit.

Not only are you honoring your own needs, but you are also respecting yourself, which permeates throughout the collective consciousness. And without any doubt, when you are authentic with your own decisions, and this propels you to be on the path of compassion for yourself and with others.

While I've been speaking about rides, this concept of cooperation and reciprocation within authentic relationships is relevant for any form of help we, as humanity, offer or need from others.

You might not be disabled or need a ride like me. However, you might eventually need emotional stability, for someone to sit beside you at the hospital. You might lose your job and need immediate assistance to support your family. As you age, you might need help with household chores. You might need help with paying bills. As human beings, we start out as vulnerable babies and children, depending on our parents or guardians. Yet, we need people, period, throughout our lives.

As my counselor once said, there are three forms of "depends" to cultivate everyday healthy relationships: 1. independence, 2. interdependence, and 3. dependence. All three are intermittently used throughout our everyday lives.

My good friend Tom is a perfect example of an authentic relationship in action. In October of 2018, there was an art gallery open house event about twenty-five minutes from my home. I asked my friend Sarah if she'd like to go with me. She accepted and asked, "Amla, is it possible for you to get a ride to the gallery? I would be happy to drive you home afterwards."

"Sure, I will definitely try to find a person to drive me to the art opening," I replied.

I searched through my contact list and saw Tom's name. I met Tom and his wife, Jan, at the same yoga center I met Joy. The added bonus was that Tom, Jan, and I live in the same town, so I instantly thought he might be available to assist me.

One of Tom's admirable qualities is that he is respectful and consistent with his actions. For him, a "yes" means he's committed. And even when he delivers a "no" answer, his warm response always makes me feel at ease, and I do not take it personally when he cannot commit to giving me a ride.

I cannot assume that Tom will say yes every time, either. It's like the classic flip of a coin; heads or tails, it's a 50/50 outcome. As a person who will always depend on receiving rides, I have become accustomed to the fact that when I ask for a favor I am mentally prepared for a yay or nay response. But if I didn't ask at all, I would have a zero chance of a greater outcome. At least when I ask for a ride, I feel that I'm being proactive and being my own best advocate. And the worst-case scenario is that I cannot go to my event or destination, which is not the end of the world.

I texted Tom the day before the opening, asking if he was available to pick me up on Saturday at around 5:00 p.m.

Tom texted me back that Saturday morning and said, "Yes, I am available."

"Thank you so, so much. I appreciate it," I answered.

Another quality I like about Tom is that, if he's running late, which he was that day, he informs me right away. You'd be surprised how many people disregard my time, especially in this day and age, with technology making it super easy to text and indicate you are being delayed. Yet Tom is a one-of-a kind person whom I cherish as my fabulous friend.

Tom picked me up and we drove over the hills of western Connecticut where the art gallery was located. As he pulled into the gravel driveway, I said, "Thank you and see you soon at yoga class."

"Amla, is Sarah here yet?" he asked.

"No," I replied.

Tom paused for a moment, then asked, "Why don't I go in with you?"

"No, no, it's okay, Tom. I can go by myself," I replied.

"No, let me just check out the art show while Sarah is on her way," he insisted.

"You really don't have to. Please go home to your wife. I will be fine," I said.

Yet Tom being Tom, he decided to attend the gallery opening until Sarah arrived. We entered the packed gallery and made our way through, viewing the intricate art pieces. I asked Tom, "Any plans with Jan for dinner?"

"Jan and I checked out this new cookbook, and we found a great recipe for meatloaf. She and I spent the afternoon prepping it so all we have to do is drop it in the oven when I get home," he replied.

I thought to myself, *I want to be in a quality and committed relationship like Tom and Jan someday. This is something I would totally do with my significant other. How cool is that?*

That was my cue, and I said, "Please go enjoy your homemade dinner with Jan."

"Are you sure you're okay? Let me know if you need a ride home and I can come back and give you one," Tom said.

"I am fine, don't worry. Sarah will be here shortly," I graciously replied.

Right at that moment, Sarah texted me and said she would be at the gallery in five minutes. I gently patted Tom on the back, thanked him, and said my goodbyes with a pleasant smile on my face.

Sarah then arrived and we had a fantastic time viewing the local talent. About thirty minutes later, Sarah and I bounced off to another gallery in my town. At the end of our joyful evening, I received a text from Tom making sure I definitely had a ride home. I texted him back with a firm "Yes" response.

In the grand scheme of things, friends like Tom, Jan, Arlene, and Sarah are like rare gemstones: once you find one or two, treasure them. As a result, I have learned to embrace people for who they are, and I try to be authentic with them the best way I can. So, whether you find yourself with a Joy person in your life, or a Tom person in your life, there is always, always something to learn from by being all of your juicy, authentic-self.

3 Exercises to Connect with Your Authentic-Self

1. Deep belly breathing is extremely powerful.

This is a simple exercise I like to do when I need to "take pause" or relieve stress:

1. Sit or lie flat in a comfortable position.
2. Place your right hand on your heart and your left hand on your belly.
3. Take a deep breath in through your nose, and exhale with a long sigh out of your mouth.
4. Inhale and count one, two, three, four (with a pause in between counts).
5. Pause at the count of four.
6. Exhale, counting from five, six, seven, eight.

Repeat steps 1 through 6 and see how you feel. Good luck.

2. Positive Affirmations.

When you are being your authentic-self, it's important to connect with your inner-child. Here are some things you can do.

1. Visit your local playground and swing, use the monkey bars, or play on the slide.
2. Color.
3. "Play" outside for at least fifteen minutes. No thinking, just being.
4. Most importantly, have fun!

When you activate your inner-child, your heart naturally expands; a true testament of being your authentic-self.

3. There are seven main energy centers within the body called Chakras.

The fourth chakra is the Heart Chakra associated with the color green. All seven chakras are tethered to a seed sound. The heart chakra Seed sound is "*Yam.*"

Repeat this sound along with imagining the color green expanding and penetrating your heart. I use this one all the time, especially when I'm out in public because:

a. It's easy to remember.

b. It's something you can do any time, any place.

c. YOU are filling yourself up with love, love, and more love.

Good luck!

Self-Care, Self-Love

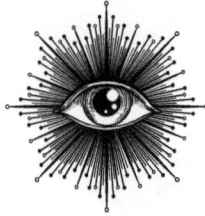

Prior to my disastrous fall and ankle break back in 2008, you couldn't pay me to exercise. Physical therapy was the one and only habitual type of exercise that boosted me up to take some much needed self-care.

That being said, after "graduating" from physical therapy, I was a fearless tiger, ambitiously taking one step at a time to get 100 percent better. I was conscientious, consistent, and disciplined. I adopted an affirmation of: "Amla, get better or don't," reminding myself that I am the solo driver of my own healing vehicle, with the final destination of being fully recovered in all four fundamental aspects of the body: the physical, emotional, psychological, and spiritual components.

I was astonished by how I had morphed from that teenage girl who cringed at the thought of yoga, to being self-motivated and engaged in physical movement. Nevertheless, as my habits changed, my whole perspective of exercise changed. Hence, I felt fabulous and exuded my brighter self by early spring.

In April I met a man named Willy through my parents' business.

He walked into our store as a customer and bought a multicolored mandala design tapestry. A week later, he spontaneously walked back into the store and asked me if I'd like to get to know him better by spending quality time together. I immediately said "yes," and for our first date I suggested that we take a stroll on the bike trail adjacent to a river in my town.

It's a majestic scenic area with the meditative sounds of rushing water flowing downstream, surrounded by picturesque timberline trees to the left and right of the bike trail itself.

You could inhale the earthy scents of pine and cedar just by sitting on the wooden benches, crafted from the local trees, nestled beside the trail. On any given day, walkers, runners, cyclists, roller-bladers, and dog walkers could be seen gallivanting along the bike trails that weaved and wended their way throughout our cozy little town.

Who would have thought that I, the non-athletic, last kid picked for a team in gym class, would discover an enchanting space outdoors for exercise and movement?

And even though three months had passed since I fractured my ankle, after Willy and I had walked merely a quarter of a mile I began limping terribly. After all, I was adapting to and coping with nine screws and a plate literally drilled inside of my foot.

In addition, one downfall after surgery was that I had developed severe scar tissue. Therefore, when I moved my ankle, I'd endure great flare-up and swelling. However, if I didn't move my ankle at all, my foot would stiffen and I'd experience obscene pain. Thus, I was darned if I moved and darned if I did not. Yet I chose to move every day, despite the pain, because I instinctively knew that if I wanted to heal and recover, I had to move, move, and move some more.

Nevertheless, Willy was in awe and said, "Wow, Amla, I'm impressed! You're in great pain and yet you are compelled to continue and walk with me."

I didn't think it was a big deal because I was determined to push through the pain and, more importantly, I liked the guy and was intrigued, I wanted to get to know him better while simultaneously surrounding myself in the sweet colors, sounds, and scents of nature at its best.

Who would've thought that physically healing and engaging in self-care would lead me into a chance at romance? I asked myself.

When I met Willy for the first time, walking was my benevolent addiction. I would "walk my ankle" for at least thirty minutes a day, five times a week. And, as I gradually increased my walk time, I naturally excelled and felt robust. All I did was walk, walk, and walk all over town. Walking not only raised my endorphins, it enabled me to increase self-confidence and self-empowerment for my "Amla well-being."

In due time, because walking was my prime form of exercise, I easily lost about ten pounds. Prior to my ankle break, I was at least twenty pounds overweight due to self-loathing, binging on sugary food, and being addicted to chips and chocolate during those debilitating depression years.

Willy and I dated from April to September of 2008. I eventually ended the relationship three weeks before I met Michael due to his aggressive personality. Even the dramas, traumas, and after-effects of the Michael situation could never deter me from my first and foremost priority of being submerged in my own self-care.

As a result of experiencing heavy heartache, especially during and after my difficult depression years, my immune system was significantly depleted. I distinctly recall my breathing becoming soft and shallow. More so, I was inhaling from the throat area versus taking full, deep, belly breaths. As a result, I was in major fear-land, and I held my breath, literally. In fact, I became quite familiar with holding, tightening, and gripping my entire body due to the severe fear secreted inside the cracks and crevices from within. Essentially, this made it impossible to escape from the vortex of anxiety relentlessly spinning throughout my mind, body, and spirit.

That being said, because I have experienced the lowest of all lows, I can confidently say that depression goes beyond the state of sadness, sorrow, or "getting over" the despair in a day or two.

Furthermore, depression is a deceptive and ruthless form of rage upon yourself. More so, it leaves you somewhat delusional and unstable, convincing you that nothing is working for you, nothing. And that's exactly why the saga of depression prolongs and continues to accumulate until you are ready to confront the fear that relentlessly bangs on your door until you choose to help yourself.

Because I had hit "rock bottom," there was no other choice but to unpeel the layers of grief that creeped, seeped, and settled their way inside of me. Ultimately, the snowball effect of heartaches and breaks had robbed me from being my authentic Amla-self.

Recap: Being diagnosed with Gyrate Atrophy, losing my driver's license, facing cataracts in my twenties, suffering from heartbreak and people stomping on my personal boundaries as a legally blind lady. In addition, I experienced full-force ignorance and discovered who my real friends are *because* of my visual impairment.

All of these extreme, growth-spurt experiences were emotionally and mentally caged inside of my body. Paradoxically, fracturing my ankle served as the catalyst to shake up my body literally, like creating a mixed drink concoction. That being said, I needed to "die" to become alive again as a form of self-resurrection.

And *because* I only walked as my first and foremost exercise, a couple of years later, I reached an exercise plateau. Therefore, I yearned for a *new* form of exercise that integrated more breathwork with quick and swift movement.

In 2010 I was introduced to Tai Chi, a soft form of martial arts that involves moving and swaying your entire body, using the breath, and creating a graceful, intricate dance with yourself.

I will never forget one of the key transformational poses that the teacher offered as a warm-up exercise. In his own words, it was called "Dump the Garbage."

This specific exercise involves standing hip-width, feet apart, with the hands resting on the sides of the thighs. You begin by taking a deep inhale while the arms float up, reaching towards the sky. Next, with a long exhale out of the mouth, along with the intentional sound of "Ha," the arms fold over and down to the ground. The class repeated these motions at least five times. And because I was fully engaged in this type of exercise, I allowed myself to surrender and release anything and everything that no longer served my highest good.

Hands down, it was an incredible way to detox from any emotional and psychological debris still drifting through my energetic auric field within my past harrowing trials and tribulations.

Soon after I experienced that Tai Chi class, I spent the next two years investing in quality time befriending and reinventing my shiny self by walking, hugging trees, being out in nature, and attending sound healing events. Essentially, I participated in any activity that made my heart smile, and I genuinely enjoyed the free-spirit feeling of radiating my authentic-self. As a result, brighter days were on the horizon and streamed through the portal of my fresh new "Amla-self."

Although, I must admit there was still some residual fear squeezing its way through me like a parasite gnawing and eradicating the immune system. Nonetheless, I was filled with trepidation that I'd plunge right back down into the old, unproductive, and toxic ways of "Amla-living" by not taking any self-care.

In January 2013, we shut down the family business permanently. Only one month later, my healing journey swung into full gear because I saw an ad for a thirty-day trial of unlimited yoga for only thirty dollars.

It's the dead of winter in Connecticut. What better way to start the new year than with the potential of a new and improved Amla? I thought to myself.

I will never forget my first experience of yoga class. I signed up for a ninety-minute "Yoga and Meditation" evening class. I was the first one out of five people who checked into the studio. There were a few people who parked their yoga mats in the back row and a few near the wall, which left a wide open space in the center of the room just for me. I figured I'd settle my mat in the front row so I could see the instructor's poses without too much difficulty.

I must confess, I was nervous. As you might have guessed already, I am more comfortable exercising alone due to the fact that I am an introvert. However, despite my initial anxiety, I vowed to partake in this group exercise class.

The class started with a simple pearl of wisdom invocation, the instructor emphasizing that yoga is not only practiced on the mat but off the mat. She also informed the class that yoga is considered a meditation in motion. "If you're breathing, you're practicing yoga," she said.

Shortly after, the yoga teacher guided us through gentle poses (called asanas), from child's pose into circular wrist rolls, to sitting in a "L" position and gently folding over our arms to touch our toes. Then our instructor had us yoga students stand up, feet hip-distance apart, and reach up our arms to the heavens with a deep inhale, then forward fold while our arms reached down toward our toes, with a long exhale. If we couldn't reach our toes, that was perfectly okay.

The yoga teacher softly reminded us that yoga is not about touching your toes; yoga is about the practice of using the breath through movement. Whether the pose is easy or challenging depends upon each student. More importantly, one always uses the breath to serve one's highest potential through each and every pose.

As the class progressed, we were guided into a full flow of postures from reaching the arms up to the heavens, to swan diving (arms in airplane wing position) down into a forward fold touching the toes, to a jackknife pose with the hands sliding up to the knees, down to a forward-fold again, to downward facing dog, into plank, and back into child's pose.

We repeated this flow at least three times in a row. And, sure enough, halfway into the third round, I felt breathless and struggled to keep up with the class. I figuratively scratched my head and wondered how I managed to walk at least three or four miles a day for the past five years, yet I had no stamina to move my way through my first formal yoga class in a studio.

In retrospect, I didn't realize how much emotional and mental trauma had spilled over spilled over my physical body due to my deep depression back in 2010. And, by using the breath through the movement and postures of yoga, the deep emotional subatomic particles floated up to the pores of my being.

The teacher had noticed that my breathing was elevated and approached me to make sure I was okay. I was grateful for that and I continued with my practice of yoga conscientiously until the end of class. Despite the fact that I was physically and emotionally exhausted, I felt amazing. It was like I had lost an additional ten pounds of emotional weight that first day of yoga class.

Even better, I discovered that yoga was perfect for me because one doesn't need 20/20 vision to benefit from it. All I needed was an open heart to see the limitless possibilities of practicing yoga.

From that day forward, I was hooked and became a "yoga junkie," making it my "duty" to attend class at least four or five times a week. The first two years of attending yoga I chose gentle and mixed-level classes due to the excessive emotional trauma and weight I had carried for years on end.

By the latter part of 2015, I started taking more abdominal, core-base vigorous classes like Vinyasa, which enabled me to carve, sculpt, and tone my Amla-self into a secure and healthy woman.

However, a few years ago, my yoga studio offered barre classes. It's self-explanatory: students utilize a ballet-type bar, engaging in fast-paced movements tied with upbeat music. I tried my first and last class in 2018 and seriously thought I was going to pass out just thirty minutes into this high-intensity energetic workout session.

I was critical and ashamed of myself. *I have been practicing yoga for five years. Why is this barre class so unforgiving with my body?*

The truth was that I found myself holding my breath during

each challenging form of movement. And with that, because of my specific experience with the barre, it felt more like a strength training class rather than incorporating the added spiritual aspect of breath intertwined with movement, as offered through yoga.

Needless to say, the barre class didn't work for me. There is no one-size-fits-all for physical fitness. As long as you move your body thirty minutes to an hour a day, at least three times a week. This represents a basic, healthy-living lifestyle.

Yoga is about accepting your authentic-self exactly where you are in the present moment, no matter how easy or hard the yoga pose (*asana*) may be. After all, yoga is not about mastering and rolling through each pose. Yoga is like an exquisite piece of composed music. It's the space in between the notes that makes the song zing. Yoga is considered as a mindful movement work in progress to strengthen all basic components of a human being. That is, it represents the interconnection between the mind, body, and spirit.

As the yoga teachers I have encountered highlight and say, "No downward facing dog will ever be the same for the same person, no matter how many times this person practices yoga."

More importantly, one will have so-so practices and also have fulfilling practices. Similar to life in general, it's all about embracing yourself on the pleasant and unpleasant days of your life.

My personal insight: If you have a great day, practice yoga. If you have an okay day, practice yoga. And if you have a crummy day, practice yoga. Yoga is the key healing remedy to maintain a harmonious and equanimous life.

Yoga enabled me to accept the fact that, regardless of what's going on externally, I have the ability to do something tangible and accessible that jump-starts my heart and daily life. Yoga is my die-hard passion to practice the benefits of movement, meditation, and being spiritual, all in one package.

And yes, practicing yoga represents my self-care gift to myself. After all, nobody can quench your own thirst except you, yourself. Half the battle of self-care is being motivated and determined to nourish your optimum well-being.

Furthermore, I learned and accepted the fact that there's always somebody who's going to be stronger, wiser, and more spiritual than me, and another person who will not be as proficient as me. Therefore, the only person I can nurture and take care of on all levels is me, my-self, and I. That being said, focusing my attention on my own needs is not selfish, it's self-full.

I must confess, yoga also has infringed upon my human so-called "weaknesses" as well. For instance, I always questioned and contemplated why the majority of my class was able to balance im-peccably in "tree pose" while I non-verbally ripped myself apart, asking myself, *Why am I toppling all over the place?*

No matter how hard I tried, I never improved through any bal-ancing poses offered by the yoga instructor. Interestingly enough, in yoga, there are no verbal or physical interactions amongst the stu-dents. Therefore, who was the one judging me? I was the one judging me; I was the only one criticizing myself. Eventually I surrendered, and I've learned to fully accept the innate truth of all of me (includ-ing all the highs, lows, and in-between aspects of me). And you can do this too. Surrender to what you are capable of mastering and con-quering, and keep reminding yourself, "I do the best I can."

I also remind myself to be gentle and compassionate towards

myself, especially during challenging poses in yoga class. It's just like teaching a child how to tie their shoelaces for the first time. You don't talk harshly to a child who is learning something new for the first time. You teach and nurture the child through unconditional love, no matter how many times he or she fails.

I have upgraded my life by filling myself up with unconditional love and compassion throughout the ups and downs of life, both on and off the mat.

For example, in yoga, I might teeter-totter over the pose, but the pose doesn't define my Amla-hood. As a result, I have learned to adapt accordingly in order to get back up again in divine time, not necessarily my time.

Interestingly enough, when I practice I am in a group atmosphere, yet I am the only soul practicing the postures. That is, I practice for my "sole" individual purpose and my "soul" spiritual purpose. Needless to say, by practicing yoga in a class environment, I benefit from the best of both worlds.

Self-care is not just about exercise. Self-care is a form of integrity, self-worth, and self-respect. It's a way of filling up your own cup of love in order to pour that cup of goodness and love out to the world.

There is also a psychological benefit of self-care. Meaning, I can wholeheartedly and confidently say, "Yes I can, and I will."

In the end, it's all about tapping into your infinite potential by trying something that organically fuels your own passion and drive. Who knows? You might surprise yourself by frolicking into the infinite qualities of your true authentic self. I broke through, and so can you.

Another added embellishment of self-care is that I started attracting more like-minded, soul-tribe people that uplifted my life. More importantly, I attracted more inquisitive individuals who operated on a higher frequency and connected with me as kindred spirits.

Ironically enough, only when we, as humans, are wedged in between a rock and a hard place do we move, shift, and shimmy our way into a more abundant and prosperous lifestyle.

This whole notion of self-care is all about free will, motivation, and dedication. In my case, I needed to fall, literally, to get back up again for my highest and holiest good. And because I'm right on track, I refuse to go back to the old paradigm Amla-ways ever again.

Self-care is just that: caring for your heartfelt self. What better way to replenish your soul than by investing in that glittery iridescent being that you already are? Find something you love to do and do it as a part of self-care and vitality.

Yoga worked for me, but it may or may not work for you. Despite the fact that it might take some trials and tribulations to usher in what works for you, always remember to listen to your heart while on the path of self-care; the ultimate feeling of being refreshed, revived, and reborn. It's just like taking care of a houseplant. If you don't feed it water and let it bask out in the sun, the plant will die. Isn't your pure essence worth taking self-care?

Always remember, once you find something positive to do as a form of self-care, stick with it. Don't give up; and more importantly, make it a part of your daily life practice. Don't just do it for a day; do it for at least twenty-one days to create a routine habit for yourself.

The main goal to keep in mind while taking self-care is to find something accessible and achievable for you so that you won't set yourself up for failure.

For example, if your goal is to lose weight, don't go on an extreme diet and starve yourself. Start off slowly and mindfully work your way up to making healthier food choices from days, to months, to years.

On the contrary, leaping into full-force overdrive can be overwhelming and self-defeating because you could easily set yourself up to fail. Take your time, pace yourself, grow from liking to work out to loving to work out as a form of Self-care.

You represent your own beacon of light, and only you can determine how to reflect it for yourself and radiate it out to the universe. If you truly believe you can, you will. If you believe you cannot, you won't. How do you define, value, and care for yourself? You decide.

Good luck on your divine journey of taking self-care.

3 Exercises to Practice Self-Care and Self-Love

1. Exercise 1

This may sound like common sense. However, so many of us need this friendly reminder, including me:

1. Drink water, water, and more water.
2. Eat a well-balanced meal every day, three times a day. Meaning, receiving enough intake of protein. In addition, receive a sufficient amount of fruits and vegetables.
3. Sleep. Try to maintain six to eight hours of sleep a day.

Remember to make this a daily practice and effort just like brushing your teeth. Good luck.

2. Exercise 2

In this day and age, the majority of people have the addictive "need" to be busy all the time, especially with technology being so accessible at the touch of a button.

Again, I cannot stress this enough for self-care: make quality time for YOU! Meaning, shutting off from the outside world, including electronics, internet, phone, people, etc. Take time to learn something new for your own vitality. For instance,

1. Take an art class.
2. Take a cooking class.
3. Spend quality time at the library reading an actual physical book.

EYE WITH A VIEW

Do something that nourishes your heart and soul. Trust me, you'll feel like a brand-new you, each and every day. Good luck.

3. Exercise 3: try any type of physical movement to get yourself out of your head.

1. Listen to music and dance.
2. Join a gym.
3. Go for a walk.
4. Join your local recreational club, like the YMCA.
5. Practice yoga.

(These are just suggestions.)

The key is to listen to your body. Trust yourself; you know what to do. Good luck!

The Art
of Acceptance

In July 2002, I ended a turbulent relationship. Therefore, I experienced a significant withdrawal phase, hindering me from living a fresh and bountiful life again. As a result, attempting to be productive in any everyday task or activity felt burdensome.

One day the following month, I remember craving a "transformational getaway" due to my roller-coaster emotional and psychological state of being.

I had an instant flashback, reverting back to the beginning of 2002 when my mom suggested that I experience "Vipassana," a meditation practice based on Buddhism. My parents experienced this particular ten-day silent retreat a few times in the late '80s and early '90s. Soon after my two-minute flashback, I logged online and plugged into the Vipassana website: www.dhamma.org.

While reading the basic overview of this type of meditation, I was fascinated by the definition of Vipassana: "Vi" means "in" and "passana" means "sight." Therefore, the full meaning of Vipassana is "insight." How ironic is that? There I was, living with Gyrate

Atrophy, and I serendipitously zoomed into a meditation practice that means insight.

Merely by reading the content online, I was more than ready to be a participant at this ten-day silent retreat. Yes, Amla Mehta would endure pure noble silence for ten days. I laugh at myself because I enjoy communicating and engaging in spiritual conversations, especially when the subject of interest fulfills and satisfies my soul essence.

The closest Vipassana retreat center happened to be an hour and a half north of my front doorstep, located in Shelburne Falls, Massachusetts. Vipassana is offered at numerous venues (including prisons) dispersed throughout multiple countries all over the world.

To my surprise, when I proceeded to sign up for the next upcoming ten-day silent retreat, set in late August 2002, the Vipassana retreat was completely booked. However, I was motivated to wait for the next available vacant time slot, which was set in late September 2002.

In what felt like a hop, skip, and a jump of time, I was finally off on this new venture to nowhere land, where we would sequester ourselves for personal growth and enlightenment within the secluded woodlands of New England.

When I arrived, I'll never forget the stunned looks on the faces of these men standing adjacent to the main entrance as I rolled in with my overstuffed suitcase. What can I say? As a woman, I needed to be prepared and immersed in the practice of Vipassana rather than worrying about doing boring chores like laundry. So, what the heck, I brought almost my entire wardrobe in order to be fully prepared for the ten-day experience.

One of the most influential factors that prompted me to be a part of Vipassana was that all vegetarian meals, lodging, and exclusive teachings provided by S. N. Goenka (the teacher/guru) would be offered based on any single donation, big or small. And because of this generous way of running and establishing the facility, nobody would be prohibited from attending the Vipassana retreat due to lack of funds.

Furthermore, when I graciously tried to give my personal contribution the first day of the retreat, the humble volunteer who had greeted me said, "Thank you, but you can give your donation at the end of the ten-day silent retreat."

"Holy wowness, I am blown away. Most meditation retreats require the participants to pay in advance," I replied.

I burst out with such gratitude, not only for this divine opportunity, but because in my perception, offering the public such a life-changing experience for any given contribution was an act of pure faith in humanity (set forth by S. N. Goenka). Meaning, all beings were warmly welcomed and accepted at any Vipassana retreat center facilitated by S. N. Goenka. Short and sweet, Vipassana is a win-win experience.

I approached the main desk to check in and inquire where I would call "home" for the next ten days. The woman greeted me with a contagious smile and guided me to my living quarters where I would share an open, spacious room with five other women.

At any Vipassana retreat, if one plans to participate with a partner of the opposite gender, you are placed in segregated living quarters: men with men and women with women. Therefore, each partner can individually and separately practice Vipassana on a sole and a soul level.

Nevertheless, I quickly adjusted to my new living arrangement by making my twin-size bed. I tucked in smooth, soft sheets, along with flannel blankets nestled underneath my plush lavender comforter. And shortly after settling into my personal space, I felt my shoulders align and reset into their natural, relaxed position by standing with my back against a wall. Needless to say, I automatically felt comfortable and at home.

For all intents and purposes, I was there to explore the internal and external pieces of my authentic-self without any added layers of self-judgment or preconceived notions. I was super eager to be and feel free, and perhaps endure life-changing experiences in such amazing ways I could only imagine.

The volunteers at Vipassana informed the new student "meditators" that all the participants were allowed to verbally communicate with each other until the first session discourse gathering in the main meditation hall soon after dinner. Not long after the first official segment of orientation, I took a deep breath in, sighed it out of my mouth, and was ready for dinner.

When I entered the dining hall for the first time, the volunteers and assistant faculty members had set up five or six rows of long, rectangular tables in the center of the room. On the sides and corners of the dining hall there were another set of tables and chairs deliberately facing the wall. At first, I found this peculiar. However, I soon realized that because this was a silent retreat, it was probably most beneficial for me to face the wall while dining to deter myself away from any distractions, including other people.

With that, the first night I devoured the delicious vegetarian dinner, which included a fresh garden salad with cucumbers, carrots, tomatoes, and fresh greens served with homemade sweet-and-sour dressing, Basmati rice (the most popular brand of rice in India), with a complimentary spicy lentil soup.

In addition, the volunteers and servers provided water and a variety of teas, including my favorite, Bengal tiger tea, to wash down the spicy, sweet, and succulent flavors of the meal.

After dinner, I washed up and prepared myself for my first discourse gathering within the main meditation hall. I quickly grabbed the handwoven, earth-toned, mossy green shawl from India. The shawl held sentimental value because my mom had offered me this soothing gift to wrap around my shoulders during the practice of Vipassana meditation. As I caressed the shawl against my tender cheek, I transcended right back to my home sweet home, since the shawl had been nestled deep inside the bottom right-hand corner of my suitcase.

At last, my time had come for the ten-day Vipassana meditation to begin. I walked over to the main meditation hall with the other women meditators and entered the front room. Thereafter, we took off our shoes and silently waited for the volunteers to queue and guide us inside. I easily distinguished the first-time Vipassana meditators like me, because they appeared perplexed yet anxious with their foreheads wrinkled and visible stress lines. (I had better vision back in 2002.)

I then habitually started to twirl my hair to calm my "Amla nerves" from being immersed in something unfamiliar and brand new, which was exciting yet terrifying at the same time. Some women fixated on and looked down at the ground, while others appeared dazed and confused. I couldn't help but wonder what thoughts were running through these other meditators' minds. With that, it was time to listen to the volunteer's instructions.

Prior to entering the main hall, we had been instructed to walk toward the assigned seating area provided for every individual meditator. In the blink of an eye, I was freaked out because the entire meditation hall was dimly lit and pitch dark.

My assigned volunteer gently escorted me by linking and locking my left arm into her right arm. Finally, I had arrived at my designated seating area. I reached toward the square cushion on the floor and scrunched myself down to the ground, sitting in the familiar "lotus" crossed-legged position.

These were the days before Miss Sophia Cane, my best friend for life. Therefore, it was quite challenging being mobile in a foreign place while coping with tunnel vision and remaining silent for ten days.

As cited on the Vipassana website and reinforced by the teacher, S. N. Goenka, there would be no writing materials, no hand gestures, no eye or human contact with one another during the entire ten-day silent Vipassana retreat. Due to the fact that this retreat was held in complete silence, the other meditators were obviously unaware of my eye condition. Hence, I felt extremely apprehensive.

I couldn't help but think, *What if I have a "people accident," a head-on collision with another meditator due to my kaleidoscope vision?*

Although right then, I calmed my nerves by telling myself, *Amla, accidents happen. In the end, I cannot control how people react or respond to my visual impairment.*

As soon as I settled into my individual space, there was a natural feeling of balance and equilibrium swirling through the frequency of the room. As a second nature gesture, I closed my eyes while I listened to the Zen sounds of silence and patiently waited for the orientation to begin.

The discourse started with an elderly person's voice conveying specific instructions through the sound system. The voice belonged to S. N. Goenka himself. He resided in India and was not present for my retreat. However, the entire Vipassana meditation teachings were relayed to the meditators via audio or video recordings.

Within the first fifteen minutes of the hour-long discourse, S. N. Goenka reinforced the code of conduct, emphasizing that noble silence is mandatory for all students practicing Vipassana meditation. That is, pure silence was imperative and served as a prerequisite for greater awareness and consciousness.

He then guided all students through a daily schedule. A typical meditation day consisted of being "gonged" awake at approximately 4:00 a.m. to meditate in the main hall, followed by breakfast. All mandatory group meditations were located in the main hall, and regularly enforced three times a day. Between all gatherings, all attendees were encouraged to practice and continue to meditate, meditate, and meditate.

In a nutshell, from 4:00 a.m. until 8:00 or 9:00 p.m., it was a persistent, disciplined continuum of being absorbed within silence while practicing Vipassana meditation. And in my eyes, this particular meditation was a life-altering, deep spiritual quest made just for me.

S. N. Goenka strongly expressed that, even when the ten-day silent retreat is over, in his own words, "Do not discuss any specific steps of the actual practice of Vipassana with anyone."

That being said, as a Vipassana student, I am not at liberty to explain or discuss any specific details of my individual meditation practice. After all, one's experience is always original and extraordinary in and of itself. Ultimately, if one desires to explore the

Vipassana meditation, one can choose to experience it by signing up and attending a ten-day silent retreat for themselves.

I wholeheartedly knew I was divinely guided and meant to be at this particular retreat. Nevertheless, I was super excited to be a first-time participant of Vipassana.

S. N. Goenka also reinforced, "You are here to work. Just because you are silent doesn't mean you are here at this Vipassana retreat to be lazy or allow time to pass by aimlessly. Within these ten full days, all meditators must practice with discipline, patience and persistence."

He ended the first orientation and all meditators were off to walk back to the living quarters and head into bed.

The next morning, I heard the faint sound of the gong at 4:00 a.m. Due to the multiple women sharing personal space, I was delayed in my morning routine because of the long line to use the bathroom and brush my teeth. When I finally had my chance to occupy the bathroom, I looked in the mirror and whispered, "This is weird," to myself. These were the only three words I had spoken aloud the entire duration of Vipassana. For all intents and purposes, I could "hear" the frequency of tranquility within the sound of silence.

In hindsight, being submerged in complete silence made me laugh at myself because there were no ramifications whether one brushed their teeth, showered, or wore fresh new clothes every day. Nonetheless, as long as you were being a proactive participant of Vipassana, personal hygiene was optional. With that, I quickly realized I didn't need my mega-suitcase of clothes after all. All I needed was me, myself, and I to practice Vipassana.

The main purpose behind this ten-day silent retreat was to experience an internal journey of tapping into the "awareness button" within my core being. And by using the breath, I maintained harmony and balance from within. More importantly, just by observing, sensing, and feeling the breath, I was seamlessly in the present moment at that time, meaning "The Now."

Days one and two of Vipassana were the most disjointed, stagnant, and strenuous days of this full-blast mode of meditation. Sure enough, I found myself subtly transcending into a decent slumber while meditating because, during Vipassana, keeping the eyes closed at all times was required for all meditators.

As a result, I had my own share of hardships with meditating for endless hours, day in and day out. There were actual moments when the passage of time became surreal, as if time felt distilled. In addition, while the parameters of my so-called "reality" gradually tapered off, I became hyper-aware; I became deeply conscious and overly aware, consistently speculating about and questioning my true purpose.

I even surprised myself that my ability to be attuned and aware skyrocketed due to the internal investigation of myself during the practice of Vipassana.

In retrospect, refraining from any verbal communication was an absolute no-brainer. That is, because nobody was allowed to communicate, nobody talked to me; therefore, it was super easy not to speak with anyone else.

By day three and four, I was making substantial progress by consciously getting acquainted with my physical environment. Although, I was still physically challenged in gaging the footpath trail leading in between my living quarters and the main meditation hall, especially at night due to my night blindness. Nevertheless, I was determined to maneuver my way through the walking path, which I successfully accomplished, moment by moment, one step at a time.

Hands down, Vipassana was one of the most profound meditation practices I have ever experienced in my entire life. Interesting fact: there are no mantras or visuals to divert one's attention during Vipassana. Hence, one uses the pure breath as their number one tool in order to practice this particular type of meditation.

As S. N. Goenka says: There is No Christian breath; no Jewish breath; no Muslim breath; no Hindu breath; no Buddhist breath. Breath is just that, breath. More importantly, breath represents the purest form of life. If you have a heart and are breathing, all beings from everywhere are welcome to practice Vipassana meditation.

Days four through seven reminded me of everyday life. There were times I felt like I was on top of the world, soaring like an eagle, while other times I felt warped, defeated, and living on autopilot, plodding my feet from my living quarters to the dining hall to the meditators' main hall where we persistently practiced Vipassana. There were moments I felt so lethargic I would have crashed on the floor within the main meditation hall if that was an option.

However, by days eight and nine, S. N. Goenka motivated us Vipassana students by offering some excellent words of wisdom. He suggested that, just because the retreat was nearly finished, we should not assume it was acceptable to ease away from the actual practice of Vipassana.

"You have come here to work persistently, with patience throughout each and every day of this ten-day silent retreat," S. N. Goenka said.

He also reminded all meditators that there shouldn't be any

harsh or irrational judgments as to what transpired over the past seven or eight days of practice. Meaning the past is just that: the past. He also stressed that just because we had one or two days left, this was the true gift of the present (without any judgment, attachment, or aversion to the outcome).

Due to those insightful words of wisdom, I practiced, practiced, and practiced, which was the most exhilarating feeling of all, especially during the final stretch of this Vipassana retreat.

The tenth day had arrived, which was bittersweet. On the one hand, I couldn't believe that ten days had come and gone in such an almighty silence. On the other hand, I was not ready to depart from the teacher, S. N. Goenka, the meditation practice itself, nor the serene and Zen living environment.

S. N. Goenka was one of the most compassionate and loving beings, greatly reminding me of a grandfather figure. The last words he said via audio were, "May all beings be free, may all beings be at peace, may all beings be happy."

With that, I sobbed away silently, attempting to divert any attention away from myself. I was deeply touched by S. N. Goenka's words, teachings, and the whole in-depth practice of the ten-day Vipassana meditation. More so, I was beyond speechless after that final discourse via audio. As a result, being allowed to speak again felt strange and abnormal because my "new normal" was NOT speaking at all.

And just as I had settled into the space on all levels, including adapting to pure noble silence, this retreat was over. Nonetheless, this transformational spiritual awakening was the most liberating and enlightening experience in my entire life.

I was mesmerized by S. N. Goenka; even after the audio system shut down. I sat there, eagerly waiting to hear his compassionate voice again. I missed him already.

And while S. N. Goenka had not been physically present during the Vipassana retreat, he symbolized the element of air. Air is everywhere and for everyone. He represented my thirst for spiritual nirvana. This was my slice of heaven, and I had no need to physically return home because S. N. Goenka represented home in my heart.

The art of practicing Vipassana meditation was a true "Amla eye-opening awakening," through which I attained spiritual transcendence.

As S. N. Goenka delivered through his insightful teachings, being present and observing yourself just as you are is the purest form of acceptance. More importantly, as humanity, by objectively accepting your inner-beingness, you can naturally accept all beings.

The key component to acquire true acceptance is to simply observe the true nature of yourself (you, "just being"). More importantly, allow the highs, lows, and transitions of your life to crystallize and transmute through the fluid living vessel of you. That being said, the more you accept the different shades of grey in your life (dark times, in between times, and lighter times), the more you rise, elevate, and experience true self-actualization (acceptance).

Acceptance is pure; no "should've" or "could've" thinking, just plain and simple "being." For instance, a baby doesn't choose where and when he or she cries. The baby will cry at a funeral, a wedding, in the car, in public, anywhere. And no, I'm not promoting "being a baby." I am merely illustrating how "just being" in totality implies true acceptance of yourself.

And by being your natural, authentic self despite your physical environment, you have the perfect opportunity to accept yourself without any attachment to or detachment from "what is" or what it's "supposed" to be. You are simply being the purest form of yourself: unconditional love.

As I mentioned earlier, the term Vipassana means "insight." With that, the key factor to living a liberating lifestyle is to see from the heart, not from the mind or physical eyes. After all, physically seeing is merely an illusion, obscuring the infinite truth of who you really are: pure love.

I was destined to experience my first Vipassana silent retreat after both cataract surgeries and prior to my depression years in my thirties. Without a shadow of a doubt, Vipassana represented personal spiritual "boot camp" training for the rest of my life.

More importantly, by practicing Vipassana meditation, it has helped me tremendously throughout this journey of facing vision loss. For the most part, I accept myself just as I am. Me being the beautiful, vivacious, effervescent Amla, made up of "self-full" love.

Furthermore, by accepting my authentic-self the best way I know how, I have no need to prove myself to me—or to anybody else. I am divinely perfect, vision or no vision. Mind you, it took me years to accept that Gyrate Atrophy is just another layer of my so-called self. That is, being legally blind does not define me. Heck, even my own name, Amla, doesn't define me; it's just a label/title. After all, the infinite soul has no labels or names attached. We are souls living as humans that are being.

I am more than just "Amla" in this lifetime. I am a child of divinity. That being said, if I am a product of God, Source, Divine (whatever label you call it), I am 100 percent made up of unconditional love. A simple example by the late spiritual teacher and author, Wayne Dyer:

Imagine a whole, uneaten apple pie on the table. If you cut a piece and eat it, it's still sliced and eaten as an apple pie, due to the fact that it's a product that originated from the whole source, an apple. (It's not labeled as blueberry or cherry.) A parallel theme: we, as humanity, are children of divinity and are pieces of pure love because we originated from Divine, Source, God (Unconditional Generator of Love). Therefore, all beings are the product of unconditional love, because we were generated from The Whole Source—Power of LOVE. Thus, there is absolutely no way humans are separate from one another—proof that we are all One Love.

Furthermore, society can attempt to block or hinder me any which way, but what matters is how I love and accept myself, for my own spiritual evolutionary process. And by practicing Vipassana meditation, I realized that Gyrate Atrophy has given me an exceptional gift. That is, being legally blind has obliterated much of the external distractions and layers of illusion that plays a subtle role with normal 20/20 eyesight.

Think about that: The average individual physically sees and absorbs the world based on perceptions and conditioned belief systems. For instance, if two people watch the same movie, what Person A might physically "see" and/or interpret is most likely different than what Person B might "see" and/or interpret within the same movie. There is no right or wrong; it's just a perception. Essentially viewing the movie from a different angle and point of view. Symbolically an external view.

However, when you close your eyes (basically resembling a blind person) and "listen" to the soothing rhythmic beat of the heart as you consciously observe the breath, this represents the internal, infinite being of you.

THE ART OF ACCEPTANCE

Hands down, the more you exercise and practice this way of being, the more acceptance is projected out to the universe. You don't have to be legally blind like me or attend Vipassana to attain a deeper understanding of self-awareness and acceptance. The path that you choose to walk is ultimately your decision. You have to want and feel pure acceptance, in order to ingest and fully live in pure acceptance.

Out of all people, I can make any excuse in the world for not fully accepting myself due to my physical handicap, but I choose not to. I continue to project my authentic-self by embracing all of me, moment to moment. Because in the end, that's all that's guaranteed here and now, in the present. Calling a spade a spade, because we all are human, sometimes you accept yourself halfway and sometimes you are just shy of 100 percent. However, the main point is to be honest with yourself. True acceptance is never strategically calculated. The Art of Pure Acceptance of yourself means you are enough, just as you ARE.

With that, please don't judge or shame yourself when you struggle to accept yourself. After all, you only learn from your scrapes, bruises, and falls. Therefore, when you find yourself judging or being self-critical, forgive yourself and move on, one breath at a time.

The art of acceptance in totality is also a non-stop process, because if we, as human beings, were 100 percent accepting of ourselves 24 hours a day, seven days a week, we would all be wholesome, enlightened beings. The main objective is to do the best you can with the cards you're dealt, right here, right now.

Declare and make a heartfelt agreement with yourself and accept and love the blessed and beautiful being you already are. After all, if you don't accept yourself, nobody else will either. Aren't you worth the quality investment of true acceptance? Good luck!

3 Exercises to Practice Full Acceptance

1. The affirmation.

"I AM *that*, I am." Repeat this affirmation infinitely. It's a wonderful way to connect to the essence of YOU!

2. Practice being present.

As Buddha, the enlightened one, said, "Be Here, Now." Practice being in the Present moment. Yes, sometimes this is easier said than done. However, make it simple. A powerful affirmation: *I am being...now.* And practice like so:

Inhale: "I am being."
Exhale: "Now."

Practice this form of meditation as much as your heart desires. Trust me, it works anywhere and everywhere.

3. Full acceptance.

Just to reiterate, full acceptance integrates the shadow parts of you, the lighter parts, and the in-between parts of you. Therefore, learn to embrace every bite-size piece of you by expanding your heart.

When I was down in the dumps during my depression, I would log on to www.youtube.com and plug in "Heart frequency" music (just as an example). The key is to invite music that lightens and brightens up your heart.

Soft Meditative Music is my easy and effective tool to help soothe the heart and soul. I listen to instrumental music at least thirty minutes a day. Good luck!

My Third-Eye Superpower

In December of 2018, I was scheduled to visit my low vision eye doctor provided by the Bureau of Education and Services for the Blind through the state of Connecticut. The main purpose of my visit was to receive new reading glasses offered to low vision patients like myself; I had been using them after both of my cataract surgeries back in 2001. This was one of my most anticipated days because I wore reading glasses for the majority of my time writing this book, *Eye with a View*, and several other writing projects in my past. That being said, I called good ole Frank, my doctor-visit driver, to take me to Dr. Kinkade's office about half an hour away from my home. When I arrived, the receptionist guided me into the waiting area. I sat there for a whopping two minutes before Dr. Kinkade called out my name (the all-time record for the shortest wait, EVER, at any eye doctor appointment).

I immediately stood up and proceeded to walk into the exam room. "I am so excited to finally receive these much needed reading glasses, Dr. Kinkade," I exclaimed.

"Well, I'm happy to make this happen for you," he replied.

While he prepared and cleaned the lenses, making sure the rims of the glasses conformed symmetrically around the curves of my face, I asked, "Dr. Kinkade, recently I have been experiencing fuzziness around the corner edges of my eyes. What do you think might be the problem?"

"Amla, have you visited your cataract surgeon recently?" he asked.

"No, why?" I curiously asked.

He continued, "Due to your cataract surgeries, some patients develop residual film on the lens of the implants. This causes blurriness or more excessive visual impairment. I recommend you schedule an appointment to see your cataract surgeon to receive an extensive eye examination."

"Okay, Dr. Kinkade. Will do," I replied.

With that, he had me read a few lines in a book to accurately check my reading abilities while I sampled my new reading glasses.

As a result, I passed all the eye tests with flying colors.

"Amla, your reading ability is just as good as it was three years ago when I last checked your vision," he said.

Wow, I thought to myself. *Rave reviews from an eye doctor. This is the first outstanding compliment pertaining to my vision in my entire life.*

Dr. Kinkade then wished me well, and I was on my way home, thrilled that I had finally received my new pair of reading glasses.

The next day, I called Dr. Gilbert's office, the same surgeon who performed both of my cataract surgeries. And when I reached Dr. Gilbert's assistant, Shirley, I promptly asked, "I was wondering when the next available appointment is to schedule an exam with Dr. Gilbert?"

"April of 2019," she replied.

"What? Four full months from now is the next available appointment?" I asked with concern.

"Yes," she said.

"Okay, well, I have no choice. I will book that date," I replied.

Flashback: three months prior in September of 2018. Figuratively speaking, I was this huge ball of hot flickering fire, well on my way to crafting this book with such zest, passion, and purpose. It was as if my high-priestess power showered all over me, symbolically representing my inner-light to penetrate my insight and share it with the rest of the world. I was flowing with words that automatically whispered in my ear, tapping into my ancient Amla-wisdom, which included the gifts of insight by enduring less physical sight.

Fast forward to after Dr. Kinkade's visit; one day in March of 2019, my mom and I decided to go for a quick trip to the grocery store. As my mom was driving, I noticed a delayed, slow-motion response. That is, within my Amla eyes, the traffic lights appeared faded in color changing from green to yellow to red. It was as if I were "catching" the light intermittently turning colors on a "hit or miss" level. Needless to say, I was terrified because I had never physically seen this way before.

I thought to myself, *Maybe it's just this one time and I am overreacting prematurely.*

Although, within the upcoming days, my central vision was noticeably compromised. That is, I would wake up seeing cloud-like shapes of hazy fog within my central field of vision. However, I was determined and driven to finish this book for my all-time accomplishment in Amla history. And in April 2019, I finished the first draft of the manuscript, exactly ten days prior to my eye appointment with Dr. Gilbert.

In all honesty, it felt so surreal achieving my ultimate dream, implanted within my heart and soul back in 2011. And now it had finally come into fruition in 2019.

April 11, 2019, is another day that would forever be engraved in my brain for the rest of my life.

No fail, I was in a tizzy regarding this particular visit at Dr. Gilbert's office. Just like a little kid, I was terrified of the unforeseen circumstances from re-examining the physiological effects of my particular vision twenty-nine years after being diagnosed with Gyrate Atrophy.

So once again, Frank, my driver, picked me up for another lovely ride to the eye doctor's office, the story of my life. On the car ride over, I proactively repeated the affirmation, "Let Go, Let God," activating my Amla inner beam of light. More importantly, I reminded myself that I cannot control the results of this eye exam nor the future outcome of this debilitating eye disease, Gyrate Atrophy. My whirlwind of emotions circled around me like a raven seeking out its prey. However, I marched forward to my own heartbeat with conviction, willing to face the outcome of my upcoming eye exam, whether it be positive or negative.

When I arrived at Dr. Gilbert's office, there was a wait for at least forty-five minutes. Just enough time for me to dwell upon the overwhelming fear of heartbreaking results. Despite this, I continued to shower myself with self-love and compassion.

At last the technician casually walked into the waiting room and announced my name. I shot up and sprinted forward with her into the examination room. As I settled myself down into the exam chair, the technician proceeded to set up for the standard procedure for me to undergo the glaucoma test, which measures the pressure of the eyes. Next, I read the standard eye chart and barely read the second line due to major glare issues in each eye. (Yes, yet again, the "g" word...glare issues.) Shortly after, the technician attempted to make my view sharper by handing me an eye gadget to gaze through the pinholes. Unfortunately, this made little or no difference to improve my central vision. And lastly, the technician dilated my eyes and guided me back into the waiting room where I sat for another twenty-five minutes. As usual, this team of ophthalmologists had very limited time during the eye examination itself. Therefore, I had prepared all of my questions for Dr. Gilbert well in advance.

While waiting, I inadvertently held my breath because, realistically speaking, I am forty-five years old. And just to reiterate, the prognosis of major vision loss is between the ages of forty-five and sixty while coping with Gyrate Atrophy. Thus, with good reason, I was uptight about the forthcoming results from this specific eye exam.

Right then, the doctor's assistant called out my name, and I proceeded to enter the exam room. I walked a few feet and sat in the examination chair smack dab in the center of the room.

Dr. Gilbert is another matter-of-fact and forthright type of eye doctor. However, he is an excellent ophthalmologist and surgeon who executes his area of expertise with great efficiency and precision.

I was tense and worked up so I anxiously asked, "Dr. Gilbert, I currently see like viewing through morning mist hovering over a body of water, like a lake. Do you think I might have developed residual film on my implants surgically inserted by you?"

Dr. Gilbert listened to me, but due to strict time constraints, he continued with the exam while speaking aloud in "ophthalmology jargon language" to his assistant who recorded data for him. This all unfolded while Dr. Gilbert directly shined high beam lights in my eyes.

"Amla, your implants from cataract surgery are perfectly clean and clear. I am afraid you are seeing through thick steam due to your eye condition, Gyrate Atrophy," he said.

I was speechless. My chronic itching fear was now my new reality. I had lost substantially more central vision, and there was no way to erase this jarring and heartbreaking news. This "blindness thing" was smashed into my face and I was figuratively losing my own fist fight to see. I was utterly devastated.

During the rest of the eye examination, I felt zombie-like and befuddled. I had lost valuable physical vision that was irreplaceable.

After the exam, I sluggishly walked out of Dr. Gilbert's office into the lobby, hunkered down, and burst into tears. I was helpless and horrified at my life-changing circumstances.

On the heels of officially discovering I had lost more vision, for approximately one month, I endured a mini-depression. Basically, I needed my own personal time and space to grieve and mourn the partial death of my vision. Yes, losing my eyesight was, and still is, inevitable. However, the closer you are to the end of something, the more angst and queasiness you feel knowing that this irreversible eye disease is inching its way right toward you. Of course, I am not the only person facing blindness. However, there is only one imprint of me, Amla. Nobody can say it's okay when it is point-blank not okay. And just because I have evolved and grown with Gyrate Atrophy, doesn't mean that the ripple effects of pain and suffering disintegrate in a New York minute. With that, I need to move through my individual grieving process at my own pace as I mourn the death of another precious part of my vision. Hence, I wholeheartedly know that there is no expiration date on when I will get through this particular difficult time in my life. Keywords: "get through something," because you never really get "over anything"; you get through, just like facing the eye of a hurricane. You can run and/or hide, but the storm is fast, fierce, and furious. More importantly, just like facing the storm, one must ride out his or her emotional or mental distress in order to get through the hardship itself (the storm).

And because of all the other heartbreaks and challenges depicted within this book, I needed to release in peace, within my own space. This included bawling my eyes out, sulking, and moping around like a lost puppy dog all throughout April and into May of 2019.

And while I acknowledge people mean well when they say, "Oh, Amla, you knew this was coming."

My impulsive reaction?

"No, you did NOT just say that."

It's like attempting to comfort somebody in New York City when a blizzard is coming. You can prepare all you want with shovels, snow blowers, mittens, and scarves. However, when the blizzard finally arrives, only then can you make your personal assessment of how you will maneuver your way out of the beast-like blizzard by digging deep to remove the excessive snow from sidewalks, driveways, and vehicles. This is similar to living with Gyrate Atrophy. I was diagnosed twenty-nine years ago. Of course I knew blindness was within my distant future. However, I am losing my vision piece by piece, year by year, and now I literally see through a haze like thick steam after a shower, anywhere and everywhere I turn my head. Of course, this is all way too intense for me to "just accept" at the drop of a hat. This is exactly the reason I choose to meet my own "Amla fear" smack in between my eyes. I remind myself that this too shall pass, although sometimes it's easier said than done.

I sought refuge by creating my own "Amla cave" and barricading myself in my bedroom for nearly one month. My parents and sister were heavily concerned. However, I spoke my truth and authentically told them, "I will get through this on my own time and within my own space."

Don't get me wrong, I'm sincerely grateful that my friends and family care so deeply and support me. And they, too, yearn to somehow shield all the pain and suffering away. However, I am the one living with gradually losing my vision. I need to honor, accept, and surrender on my own "Amla time," not anybody else's time.

In a nutshell, I took my own advice that I have sprinkled throughout this entire book, and I actively felt all of my flip-floppy emotions in order to feel, accept, and surrender to what is. I followed up with the attitude: *Oh, here's another challenge, Amla. How am I going to jump through another hoop of extreme change? And how will I move forward with my life suffering from more substantial vision loss?*

In all honesty, the one and only thing that kept my spirit high like a kite was the fact that I finished this book, period. I fulfilled my own dreams and aspirations of writing my Amla purpose book. More importantly, I have come to terms with the fact that there is more to me than meets the eye. Prior to this recent vision loss, I was capable of writing all day without any significant visual problems. Currently, writing suits me best in the morning or in the evening; nothing in between when I write using my phone. (Yes, I wrote this entire book on my phone.)

MY THIRD-EYE SUPERPOWER

I wear sunglasses even while indoors practicing yoga at the nearby studio because the glare from the windows strains my eyes. My long-distance vision is predominately shot and gone, and my nearsighted vision is stable, but I need the person to be physically two feet (maximum) away from me to see whatever I DO SEE. For all intents and purposes, I have accepted that my physical way of seeing has been compromised significantly.

In mid-May, the pinpoint portal of light started to peep through my heart and soul. My yoga practice helped me in monumental ways because this was my opportunity to focus on something purposeful by physically staying connected to my heart.

Also, my loyal and endearing friend Tom was amazingly supportive during and after my mourning period. By the latter part of this grieving process, I had an epiphany moment. I realized that by experiencing the poorest physical vision of my life, I had never felt so fresh, alive, and soulfully nourished in my entire life. I also recognized that I am a soul experiencing soul purpose by writing this book. That being said, I have achieved exactly what I sought out for myself: living and breathing the true unconditional love that I already am, vision or no vision. Without any doubt, I genuinely know from the core of my being that this was ALL a part of the divine plan.

The other subtle enriched feature of losing my vision is that I have enhanced my third-eye intuition (superpower vision). Meaning, I feel and embody the transparent truth of ALL of me: the unconditional ooey-gooey love. With that, of course I would've never "seen" and felt so profoundly from my heart without the gift of Gyrate Atrophy.

However, because I'm human, I still cannot absorb the insane possibility of not being able to physically read, see colors, or see my loved ones because I still preserve partial vision. On a positive note, it's only the peaks and valleys of hardcore experiences that paved the true meaning and richness of my Amla life. Nevertheless, I live my life with absolutely no regrets, because I've faced every battle on the field of life like a true warrior woman. Consequently, I am only a survivor because I figuratively fought for my life, on and off the battlefield. That is, even when I was benched from the fight, this was my time to rest, restore, and recalculate the next few steps in order to move forward on my Amla-path.

Ultimately, the only entity that enabled me to survive was faith in myself stemming from God, Source, Creator (whatever label you call the higher power). Despite the fact that I felt stomped on and figuratively defeated during these intense and difficult times, I somehow managed to confront my personal fears, one strike at a time.

Such is life. Only through the trials and tribulations does one learn when to fight on the field FOR your life, and when to back off, sit on the bench, and observe "the fight" from a distance. The underscore factor is that it gives you a panoramic perspective known as true insight. More importantly, even though my world of physical colors is literally fading away, paradoxically, I have richly colored my Amla-life by collecting the precious gemstones of life-lessons, wisdom, and insight along the journey of being legally blind.

People ask me all the time…

"How do you see? What do you see currently?"

Here are some examples of how I see:

Presently, any external objects, people, babies, affect my physical vision, considering I bump into things all the time. Sometimes sunglasses help, sometimes they don't because when worn, they may project too much darkness and then I cannot see efficiently. I am also extremely sensitive and negatively affected by any intense lights, whether it be the ceiling lights at the grocery store, headlights from oncoming traffic, or direct sunlight.

If you reach out to shake my hand as I am naturally conversing and directly looking at your facial expressions, I won't see your hand. Therefore, I usually extend my hand out first, so the other person's hand naturally meets mine and there are no misconceptions.

Let's say I decide to go for a walk with a friend, and he or she is parallel and adjacent to my left. If this person stops suddenly to tie their shoelaces without any verbal cues, I will continue walking and proceed forward until they yell out my name and tell me to stop. (This has happened several times.)

In simple medical terms, when I was diagnosed with Gyrate Atrophy back in 1990, I was basically capable of seeing all objects and people with a full semi-circle point of view (a full-range measurement of a 180-degree field of vision). Presently, I maintain a visual peripheral field of fifteen degrees within each eye. More so, the full radius of how I will "see" when Gyrate Atrophy progresses over time is probably seeing through the width and the size of a quarter (a currency coin in the United States). In addition, I will also only be able to detect the sun rising (in the form of dim evening light).

Ironically enough, if I had the luxury of maintaining 20/20 vision, in my perception, it's not the end all, be all. My incredible third-eye superpower vision (the sixth chakra energy center located in between the two eyebrows) runs a parallel theme to the character Dorothy from *The Wizard of Oz*. She was under the illusion that the meaning of "home" was an external force beyond her backyard in

Kansas (a state within the United States). When in reality, Dorothy's home resided in her heart. And that home, of course, existed the entire time Dorothy followed the Yellow Brick Road leading her "home." Similarly in my Amla-world: when I endured much sharper vision, I developed low self-esteem, never felt good enough, and I was insecure. Nonetheless, I didn't believe in my awesome Amla-self. Currently, with the poorest vision ever, I walk and project myself with poise, confidence, and unconditional love for myself. More importantly, I exude my "Amlahood" with an in-depth "knowingness and awareness" of who I am. And this only became apparent in my life through "seeing less." Therefore, seeing less enabled me to see from my heart. Ultimately, my spotlight laser-beam vision always existed; I merely was too blind, no pun intended, and was "looking" in the wrong direction: "outside-in" versus the purest form, "inside-out."

And now, speaking from my overflowing and full-of-love heart, I see the world with a shiny, astronomical, over-the-moon point of view. However, I cannot, and will not, forget those coal mine days, months, and years when I resided in deep darkness and despair. After all, a diamond doesn't become a diamond overnight. It has to sit through darkness, literally, to shine and beam that luminous light.

Internally, I feel like I have climbed Mount Everest, and this is my time to enjoy the sweet view. Although, because of my tumultuous path of vision loss, I will always remember that regardless of whether I'm on top of the world or not, I, Amla Mehta, was once at the bottom looking up at this enormous and treacherous mountain climb ahead of me. Ultimately, whether or not I am at the bottom, middle, or at the top of the mountain, the main point was and still IS to be all of my Amla authentic-self, wherever I may be on my personal journey of vision loss. Of course, that's easier said than done.

With that, my "real eyes" are projected from my third-eye view (the "pure light" located in between the eyebrows). This spectacular light represents a streaming white spotlight to navigate and emulate my sparkling Amla-self throughout this beautiful world.

There is a powerful saying in India: "No Dukh, No Sukh!" Meaning, without real pain, there is no real bliss. I can attest to that. I unpeeled the layers of pain and suffering moment to moment, day by day, year by year, by downright facing my fears. Who would've thought that I would be predestined to "see and be" in the dark in order to feel and "see the light"? I "see perfectly" by imperfectly physically seeing. More importantly, the frequency and current of electricity (pure light) always soared through me; I merely needed to search for the light switch within me to turn my "Amla Light" ON. And NOW it's on, and I'm never turning it off. Oh, what a feeling it is!

I thank God for all of the beautiful blessings along my enlightening life path! And of course, I thank you all for opening your hearts and minds and vicariously living through my eye-opening journey of gradual vision loss. I will sign off with my Amla original signature expression.

Shine Love, Shine Light, Shine You!
Amla Mehta

Please feel free to contact me.
You can *like* my Facebook page:
www.facebook.com/Amlainspires
amlalights@gmail.com

3 Exercises to Increase Your Intuition

1. As mentioned earlier, there are seven main energy centers in the body called chakras. The sixth chakra is located between the eyebrows (known as the third eye). The color that is directly connected to the sixth chakra is indigo. The seed sound for this chakra is "*Aum*." Chant this sound limitlessly to heighten your own intuition. Good luck.

2. Visualize swirls of white light and gold light streaming through the crown of your head through your entire being, down through the soles of your feet shooting down to the core of Mother Earth. Imagine this light washing away any impurities within your body. Remember to clean and cleanse through the white and golden light prior to the next step. Next, imagine electric blue and white light laser-beam energy shining into your eyes. These particular colors mixed together accelerate the ability to "see" from a third-dimensional view and upgrade toward the fifth dimensional eagle-eye view. Try it, it works wonders.

3. Repeat the mantra, "It's great to be me and clearly see." So simple, yet so profound. It's easy to remember. Good luck!

Acknowledgments

I'd like to honor my endearing and nurturing mom, Hira Mehta. You have supported me my entire life, and I will never forget your unconditional love for me, especially while living with Gyrate Atrophy. Jai Shri Krishna, Mummy. I love you!

I could NOT have pursued my dream aspiration of writing this book, *Eye With a View*, without my outstanding publisher, editor Emily Hitchcock of Columbus Publishing Lab. I genuinely love and adore you like a soul-sister. Thank you for being my A-mazing publisher, colleague, and true friend. I cannot thank you enough. I love you, dear Emily. Keep on shining.

I'd also like to thank my writing coach, Lori Deboer, from CO. Thank you for motivating me to strive to do my best and nothing less. Blessings, Lori.

www.ingramcontent.com/pod-product-compliance
Lightning Source LLC
Chambersburg PA
CBHW021359090426
42742CB00009B/918